The Right Road

"*The Right Road* is like 'mapquest' for anyone who wants to be a healthy leader enhancing lives. If you are thinking about having a more balanced lifestyle, this provides great directions for you. If you are headed in the wrong direction and need to make a U-turn, Dr. Halaas provides a prescription for you. If you are making plans to begin a healthier life, you'll find helpful tips and suggestions. If you are already on your way to a healthier life, you'll find inspiration (along with your perspiration) to 'fight the good fight, to run the race.'"

—Pastor Ronald T. Glusenkamp, ELCA Board of Pensions,
Vice President-Customer Outreach, and author of *Sign for These Times*

"Gwen Wagstrom Halaas's experiences as a family physician and wife of a pastor have given her a keen understanding of the many physical, emotional, and spiritual challenges facing today's clergy. She understands how the demands of ministry make it difficult for clergy to take proper care of themselves. In *The Right Road* Dr. Halaas offers valuable advice that clergy can use to enhance their own health and to lead their congregations in ministries of health and healing. This is a book that should be read by every pastor and by congregational leaders concerned about the health and well-being of clergy."

—W. Daniel Hale, co-author of *Healing Bodies and Souls:*
A Practical Guide for Congregations

Other titles in

PRISMS

The Right Road
Life Choices for Clergy

Gwen Wagstrom Halaas, M.D.

Fortress Press
Minneapolis

THE RIGHT ROAD
Life Choices for Clergy

Cover art by Heidi Younger. Used by permission.
Cover design: Zan Ceeley
Interior design: Allan Johnson, Phoenix Type, Inc.

Unless otherwise noted, Scripture quotations are from the New Revised Standard Version Bible, copyright © 1989 by the Division of Christian Education of the National Council of the Churches of Christ in the USA and used by permission.

Food pyramid on page 19 reprinted with the permission of Simon & Schuster Adult Publishing Group. From *Eat, Drink, and Be Healthy: The Harvard Medical Guide to Healthy Eating* by Walter C. Willett, M.D. Copyright © 2001 by President and Fellows of Harvard College.

Library of Congress Cataloging-in-Publication Data
Halaas, Gwen Wagstrom, 1954–
     The right road: life choices for clergy / Gwen Wagstrom Halaas.
          p. cm. — (Prisms)
     Includes bibliographical references.
     ISBN 0-8006-3657-0 (pbk.: alk. paper)
     1. Clergy—Health and hygiene. I. Title. II. Series.
BV4397.5.H35 2004
248.8'92—dc22   2004008036

This life, therefore, is not godliness but the process of becoming godly, not health but getting well, not being but becoming, not rest but exercise. We are not now what we shall be, but we are on the way. The process is not yet finished, but it is actively going on. This is not the goal but it is the right road. At present, everything does not gleam and sparkle, but everything is being cleansed.

—Martin Luther

Contents

Preface

Healthy leaders enhance lives—your own life, the lives of your family members, the lives of your congregation members, and the lives of those in your community. Being healthy and feeling healthy bring energy and joy to your own life and work. Feeling healthy helps you to be an active, loving, and engaged member of your family. Being an effective leader in your ministry requires self-care and balance to respond to the complex issues and needs of people. Being healthy and having healthy relationships enables individuals and congregations to reach out into the community to invite new members and to meet the needs of the community. Healthy leaders and healthy congregations are the sign of a vital and meaningful church in the world.

This book is an invitation to think about your own health and lifestyle. Whether you are an ordained minister or lay leader in public ministry or a faithful Christian in ministry through your vocation in daily life, it is a call to action to practice self-care and balance in all aspects of your health *and* wellness. The church is a community whose values, language, history, and relationships provide the support and incentives to change and encourage healthy lifestyles. As a faithful community, we can lead by example toward improved health.

As a family physician who has brought babies into the world, helped people die peacefully, helped many try to lead healthy lives, and counseled many with emotional and vocational struggles, my ministry is to help individuals and communities strive toward better health. As a busy professional wife of a pastor, mother to young adult children, and relative of several other Lutheran pastors, I am fully aware of the barriers and challenges to leading a healthy life. As a teacher of medical students and young physicians, I am aware of the need to lead by example and teach in a way that is practical and makes a difference.

Although fully ecumenical, this book is a product of the Evangelical Lutheran Church in America's (ELCA) Ministerial Health and Wellness Initiative, a partnership between the Division for Ministry and the Board of Pensions. This ELCA initiative started by addressing the health issues and needs of rostered leaders (clergy and commissioned lay workers).

I want to recognize the foresight and the groundbreaking work in pastoral health and wellness done by the InterLutheran Coordinating Committee on Ministerial Health and Wellness. Their awareness of the need and their hope for healthfulness in the future led to James Wind's "Letter on Peace and Good Health" and to the review of the research by the National Institute for Healthcare Research, "Physical and Mental Health Issues among Clergy and Other Religious Professionals." These works were the beginning of my understanding of the issues— theological and medical.

I want to thank Joe Wagner, Craig Settlage, and Stan Olson of the ELCA Division for Ministry and John Kapanke and Dave Adams of the ELCA Board of Pensions for their commitment to health and wellness for the rostered leaders of the ELCA. I want to thank all my coworkers from the Division for Ministry and from the Board of Pensions for their welcoming support and encouragement. I want to thank all the pastors and rostered leaders who have listened and shared their personal experiences and hopes for the future.

Thanks, especially, to Craig Settlage, Ron Glusenkamp, and Gary Harbaugh, who spent hours reading and giving helpful and friendly suggestions for the right words for *The Right Road.*

Finally, I want to thank my families who are pastors, who love pastors, and who support pastors in many ways. I want to thank them for their unending love, for their deep faith, for their patience, and for their very realistic approaches to life. Thanks to my husband, Mark, for listening and reading and loving, and thanks to our children, Per, Liv, and Erik, for always keeping me honest.

Introduction

The Right Road is designed to be a guide to understanding the fullness of health in the context of public ministry. It is directed at an audience of church leaders, ordained and lay, but is useful for anyone seeking health in the context of vocation and faith. The book includes information about health, suggestions for personal health improvement, and ideas for incorporating health into public ministry, personal and congregational. Bridging the sections on health are fictional stories about a pastor, RL, and others' fictional perspectives on his life and health. I wanted these stories to be honest and realistic without using real stories. The elements of the stories come from my experience in healthcare and caring for the health of pastors, but the names and details are all fictional.

Although research shows that religious commitment and activity have a positive impact on health, research done on ordained ministers from various churches and on rostered lay leaders identifies significant health problems that need to be addressed. These problems include the following:

1. *Stress and depression.* Self-reported survey results in 2001 from ordained ministers and rostered lay leaders of the Evangelical Lutheran Church in America (ELCA) indicate problems in the areas of job-related stress, depression, relations with family and friends, finances, and dissatisfaction with personal devotional life.[1] One published study of 250 religious professionals found that Protestant clergy had the highest overall work-

related stress and were next to the lowest in having personal resources to cope with the occupational strain.[2]

2. *Weight and lack of physical activity.* Sixty-eight percent of ELCA ordained ministers (59 percent of rostered lay leaders) report weights in the overweight or obese range, compared to 61 percent of the U.S. population. Thirty-four percent of ordained ministers (32 percent of rostered lay leaders) report weights in the obese range by body mass index (BMI) compared to 22.5 percent of the U.S. population. Contributing to this statistic, one in four of ELCA rostered leaders reported no exercise. The 2001 *Pulpit & Pew* survey on pastoral leadership of religious leaders from many different denominations and faith groups reports that 76 percent of clergy are overweight—79 percent of men and 52 percent of women.[3]

3. *Nutrition and cholesterol.* Twenty-eight percent of ELCA ordained ministers and rostered lay leaders report elevated blood cholesterol, which is similar to that of the U.S. population. About 15 percent of ELCA rostered leaders report four or more servings of fat per day, and about 30 percent report no more than two servings of fruit per day.

4. *High blood pressure and heart disease.* While the reported percentage of ELCA ordained ministers and rostered lay leaders diagnosed with high blood pressure or heart disease is comparable to rates of the U.S. population, there is still concern. A 1999 review of the health status of ordained ministers suggests that they are in the top ten occupations of people dying from heart disease, and that ordained Lutheran ministers have a higher rate of heart disease than other ordained ministers. This is supported by a high rate of claims being paid by the ELCA Board of Pensions for the treatment of heart disease.

This information about ELCA rostered leaders needs to be considered within the context of the health of other clergy and church workers and within the health status of Americans today. In 1980 a study of 28,000 male Protestant clergy of the 1950s showed that, in every diagnostic category, they lived longer than other males, including other professionals.[4] A 1999 study of the death certificates for pastors from 1982 to 1992, however, showed that clergy were among the top ten occupations to suffer death from heart disease.[5] In order to make the necessary personal and institutional changes to improve clergy health, we must understand the changes in public ministry and the changes in American culture that have led to this apparent significant change in health status.

Other studies of religious professionals found that Protestant clergy had the highest overall work-related stress and were next to the lowest in having personal resources to cope with the occupational strain.[6] A study in 1987 found that the top three stressors for clergy were congregational conflicts and church conservatism, difficulties involved in parish commitments, and the emotional and time demands of crisis counseling.[7] Researchers have found that one in three pastors leaving ordained ministry had family difficulties, and that clergy rank third in percentage among professionals who are divorced. A study of male clergy and their wives found work-related stress on the family in two areas: the lack of available social support and intrusion on family life. Finally, although clergy rank in the top 10 percent of the population in terms of education, their salaries rank only 325 out of 432 occupations.[8]

This concern about the health of our church leaders coincides with a growing concern for the health of the American public. We are living in a time of "epidemics" of obesity, heart disease, diabetes, and depression. The real causes of these diseases relate to our lifestyle. We avoid activity, eat too much "fast" or processed food, work too many hours, and are isolated from our families and friends.

The fact that many of the church's leaders are overweight, inactive, depressed, and at increasing risk for heart disease and diabetes is a real concern. Taken in the context of a church in a time of declining membership, smaller and fewer congregations, older age at ordination than previously, and decreasing numbers preparing to serve congregations, this is an urgent situation.

Addressing health and wellness effectively must involve the full professional lifespan of ordained ministers and lay leaders and must be addressed in the seminaries, congregations, and administrative units of the church. We can set an example for other churches and institutions in developing faith-hardy leaders and a healthy and flourishing church. These health issues are not unique to church leaders, but are the result of American lifestyles compounded by the unique expectations and responsibilities of ministry. We will more likely be successful if we take on this initiative as families, congregations, synods, and communities.

The Story of RL

Let me tell you the story of RL, a patient of mine whom I saw in my office recently. He made an appointment at the urging of his wife. I asked how he was doing, and he reported the following:

He has not been feeling well for quite some time and has been getting worse recently. He is not sleeping well, and he awakens early in the morning unable to get back to sleep. He awakens tired and remains tired throughout the day. He doesn't have much of an appetite, yet he has gained twenty pounds over the past twelve months. His work is stressful. He is a pastor of a Lutheran church of one thousand members and has been there for seven years. This church also has a part-time assistant pastor and three other staff members. In addition to the difficulties of keeping the position of youth director filled, he is also dealing with a church secretary who does not get along with the assistant pastor. He has also had to deal with conflict within the congregation. Most days he feels as if he is dragging himself to the church.

RL is fifty-one years old and has been married for twenty-five years to Sarah, who works part-time in a library. Their relationship has been quite good until recently. She has been concerned about RL's health, but when she tries to help, he accuses her of nagging. They used to spend time together on his day off, but he hasn't been able to have a real day off for over a year. They have three teenage children. Their son has been having difficulty in school this year, and RL expresses some concern about the friends he is hanging out with. His oldest daughter, Deborah, has expressed an interest in the ministry, but RL has difficulty mustering any enthusiasm to encourage her in that direction. In addition, RL's mother's health has been going downhill since the death of his father nine months ago. He and his wife have had to spend more time with her, taking her to clinic appointments and helping her around the house.

RL is currently taking medication for high blood pressure. His cholesterol has been in the low 200s. He has never been hospitalized. He is allergic to cats but takes no medications. He currently does not smoke, but he did smoke one pack per day until he quit ten years ago. He drinks occasionally but rarely during the week. On vacation days, he drinks up to a six-pack of beer. RL's father died from a heart attack at age seventy-three and had high blood pressure and heart problems prior to his death.

When questioned about his lack of sleep, RL admits that it has been getting worse and that some times he nods off during committee meetings at church. He sleeps about four hours a night. He awakens anxious about things in general, at home and at church. He describes having difficulty controlling his emotions but does not feel overwhelmed and is not considering suicide. He knows that he is more irritable lately, especially with his kids. RL does admit to eating when stressed—usually candy, doughnuts, or fast food. He currently is not exercising. He used to go to the gym once a week to play basketball with a community team, but he hasn't gone for over a year, since he had an episode of chest pain while playing basketball. He has a loving relationship with his wife but says that their sex life is not what it used to be—there isn't enough time and he doesn't have the energy. He spends most days in his office or car, and he usually eats and goes to bed once he gets home.

RL appeared anxious and uncomfortable in the room. He is about forty pounds overweight. His blood pressure was elevated. The rest of his exam was unremarkable. An electrocardiogram done in the office was normal. We drew blood to evaluate his cholesterol. We then had a lengthy discussion about his health. I told him that he clearly had symptoms related to stress and appeared to have signs of depression. I also told him that his blood pressure was not under control, and that his chest pain might be an indication of heart problems, especially since his father had a history of heart disease.

I expressed concern about his relationships with his family members, about his ability to continue to tolerate stress at work, about his ability to balance responsibilities at home and at work, and about his general state of health. We talked about appropriate use for antidepressant medication and agreed that, although he didn't need a prescription now, he might in the near future. I referred him for counseling for stress reduction and depression.

I increased the strength of his blood pressure medication and gave him a prescription for physical activity—walking ten minutes three times a week with a plan to increase gradually over the next six months. I gave him information on lowering cholesterol and fat in his diet and tips on how to lose weight effectively. I advised him to make specific time in his calendar for his wife and for time with each of his children while they were still around home. I told him he must schedule a vacation in the next two months and that he must talk to the church council about assuring one day off each week.

I also told RL that I needed to see him back in two weeks. I expressed concern about his health again and advised him that he must take these prescriptions seriously. With his risk for heart disease, he had to get his blood pressure controlled, improve his diet, lose some weight, and increase his physical activity. The good news is that by doing those things, his emotional state should also improve. However, we discussed the warning signs for worsening depression and discussed the need to review his work situation in the near future.

This is the fictional story of an individual, but it is also descriptive of the health issues affecting the rostered leadership of our churches—stress, overweight, physical inactivity, and cholesterol/heart disease. Just as this individual, RL, is at high risk for a heart attack and for depression that would have a serious impact on his health, his work, and his family, so is the church at high risk for the physical and emotional health of their leaders impacting the work and vitality of the church.

Questions

1. What do you think can explain the apparent change in health status for clergy in the 1950s and clergy in the 1980s (from the healthiest to being at high risk for heart disease)?

2. What do you think are the greatest stressors in public ministry?

The Wholeness Wheel

The "Wholeness Wheel" is a pictorial guide to balancing all aspects of health.[9] The wheel starts in the center with you as a new creation through baptism and a member of the body of Christ. Around the wheel are the individual aspects of wellness—physical, emotional, social/interpersonal, vocational, and intel-

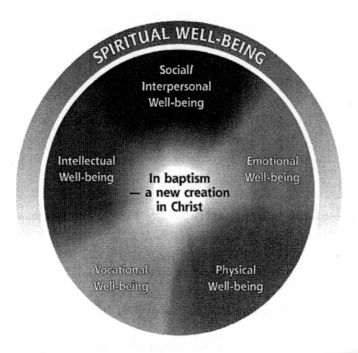

lectual. To be whole means to keep these aspects in balance by intentionally nurturing and attending to each aspect. If one area is neglected, the whole will be out of balance. Spiritual health surrounds, contains, and supports us through faith and our relationship with God.

God wonderfully creates us as physical, emotional, social, intellectual, vocational, and spiritual beings. To experience the fullest potential of what God has intended for us as individuals and as members of a faith community, we must nurture ourselves by attending daily to each of these aspects. Rest, nourishment, physical challenge, joy, empathy, love, friendship, accomplishment, peace, and devotion are as essential to our health and life as air and water. As Granger Westberg puts it, "In the Christian tradition, health is seen as an ongoing process. Good health is not an end in itself, but rather it is an enabler. It gives us the energy and vitality to serve and love others, and thus good health is seen in the context of purpose. It is a liberator."[10]

What Is Health?

We live in a society that demands and expects "perfect" health and whose medical profession has defined health as the absence of disease. As humans, we cannot be perfect, but health is clearly much more than the absence of disease. So what is health? In 2001 the Institute of Medicine published a report entitled "Health and Behavior" that used the term "positive health."[11] This term was derived from studies showing that attitudes and behaviors enhance the body's resistance to and recovery from disease, illness, and surgery. Positive health is defined as including

- a healthy body
- high-quality personal relationships
- a sense of purpose in life
- self-regarded mastery of life's tasks
- resilience to stress, trauma, and change

The report goes on to say that psychological factors, such as anger, hostility, depression, and vital exhaustion have been associated with susceptibility to illnesses such as heart disease. These emotional factors are often not considered by us as causes when we experience illness. Symptoms of excessive fatigue, increased irritability, and demoralization commonly precede heart attacks, and job stress is a risk factor for heart disease. These are not the "classic" symptoms of heart disease as determined by our physicians. Dealing with these emotions and symptoms, however, is critically important in preventing and recovering fully from the physical disease that results from emotional distress and exhaustion.

Behaviors that significantly impact health include smoking, alcohol abuse, physical activity, diet, and sexual practices. We know this, yet we don't directly tie these behaviors to the outcomes of heart attacks, strokes, cancer, or HIV. We are still in "disease mode" and function as victims of disease rather than as individuals taking a measurable risk by our behaviors. Social factors also impact health. Many studies have shown that people who do not have a supportive social network are at risk of premature death. Isolation is directly related to early death and worse health. Other studies have shown a strong relationship between economic status and income inequality and health status and mortality. That is, the lower you are on the socioeconomic ladder, the poorer your health. Additionally, if you perceive that you are being paid less than your peers, your health is negatively impacted.

One current example of the complexity of factors that have an impact on health is the increasing percentage of Americans who are overweight or obese. Being overweight is a significant risk factor for chronic diseases such as diabetes, high blood pressure, heart disease, arthritis, several cancers, depression, and premature death. Obesity is related to gender, culture, and socioeconomic status. More Americans are eating away from home, and when they do, they eat larger portions of higher calorie food that is higher in saturated fat, cholesterol, and sodium and lower in calcium and fiber. In addition, Americans are less physically active as a result of the convenience of cars, remote control devices, elevators, electronic communication, and in-home entertainment.

The problem is not that we don't know this information or that we aren't concerned about weight and lack of fitness. It is that we are "too busy," "too tired," "too stressed," and/or we "have tried and failed," "can't afford," or "will do it someday." The problem is that cues and temptations to overeat, eat the wrong foods, watch TV, or sit at the computer surround us. It is that we have competing values, such as getting the most for the least by "supersizing", not wasting by cleaning our plates, not offending by accepting what is offered, and maintaining a neat appearance by not being overly active. We may ignore, delay, or politely avoid addressing self-care until it is too late.

The Importance of Self-Care

We care for ourselves by meeting the basic needs of nourishment, comfort, rest, and social activity or contact. Our bodies and minds need healthy food at regular intervals, consistent and adequate rest, and stimulation by regular physical activity. We understand ourselves better and are happier because of our intimate social relationships. We are fulfilled in our vocation by using our talents to make the world a better place. And our relationship with God helps us lead fulfilling lives.

Making sure that these needs are met is not selfish. Help comes from God, who has given the commandment to "love the Lord your God with all your heart, and with all your soul, and with all your mind and with all your strength," and "love your neighbor as yourself" (Mark 12:30–31 and parallels; Lev. 19:18; Deut. 6:4). We often forget or deny the need to love ourselves. We will not have the warmth of heart, depth of soul, clarity of mind, or the power of strength to truly love the Lord and actively express love to our neighbors if we don't first love ourselves. If we let the Holy Spirit guide our lives and provide us with love, joy, peace, patience, kindness, goodness, faithfulness, humility, and self-control, it makes the important job of taking care of ourselves infinitely easier.

In my years of family practice, I have written many prescriptions, not just for medications, but for self-care. "Plan for and take a relaxing vacation within the next month." "Schedule a regular date with your significant other." "Walk for thirty minutes at least five times a week." "Eat three meals daily—don't forget breakfast!" I am convinced that these prescriptions, when followed as prescribed, have had a significant impact on my patients' health and allowed them to avoid the need for prescribed medications. We don't have to visit a doctor to get a prescription for self-care. It should be part of our daily routine just like brushing our teeth and getting dressed. When we do visit our doctor or clinic, questions about the quality of our sleep, our eating habits, our relationships, or our vocational satisfaction are just as important as questions about the nature of our pain or our bodily functions.

Sarah's Story: RL's Wife

I saw RL's wife, Sarah, the other day. She thanked me for seeing RL and told me that she could already see a difference. He seemed to be more attentive at home and more interested in what was going on in the family. She had been very concerned about his not sleeping well. When she heard about him having chest pain, she became afraid of losing him—like his father—to heart disease. Her eyes lit up as she told me the story of how they had first met. They had been students at the same college.

During her freshman year, Sarah signed up for a service project in the community. An older couple who attended the same church RL attended had a house that was sorely in need of attention, but they were too frail to make repairs on their own and too poor to pay someone to do it for them, so RL had organized the service project to help them out. When Sarah showed up that morning to work, there were fourteen others in the group. She had never met RL before, but she couldn't take her eyes off him the whole day.

"He was so full of energy; his enthusiasm was contagious. He was the center of attention, full of joy and laughter. He was gentle and caring with the owners of the house, encouraging them to participate where they could and introducing them one by one to each of us as we worked. He was clearly in charge of the day, organizing the work and keeping us motivated and on task. He made it fun, working alongside each one of us, getting to know us and helping those of us who were novice painters to not do too much damage. I could see that he loved what he was doing."

RL and Sarah sat together during the group's lunch break.

"He asked what I thought of my college experience so far. He was a religion major and knew that he was going to seminary. He talked about his desire to become a pastor. No one in his family was a pastor, but his own pastor had encouraged him to consider the ministry ever since his confirmation. He was part of a great youth group in his church, where he learned to know and love Christ and began to think about the meaning of life and the possibility of being a pastor. I can remember how his eyes and face lit up as he talked about it. I remember wishing that I could be as certain and as excited about the future.

"That is why I encouraged him to see you," she said to me. "I saw the light go out of his eyes. He had always loved being with people and sharing his love of Christ, but lately I could see him struggle. He had a hard time leaving in the morning, and even on Sunday he was just not the same. He spoke the words of his sermon, but the fire wasn't there. I don't think others were aware of it, but I could see him trying too hard to be warm and caring as the people left the service. His eyes used to dance; there used to be laughter and hugs. I knew I had to do something when I overheard him with our daughter Deborah. She was talking about her college classes and her growing interest in her religion courses. She said to him, 'You know, Dad, I might even think about seminary!' There was silence. I turned to look at them and caught a glimpse of that 'deer in the headlights' look on his face. He quickly said, 'Oh, sweetie, that's great.' But I knew he didn't mean it."

Questions

1. How would you describe your health in terms of the definition of positive health?

2. Describe your self-care. Has your approach to self-care changed? If so, why?

Physical Well-Being: A Healthy Body

Do you not know that your body is a temple of the Holy Spirit within you, which you have from God, and that you are not your own? For you were bought with a price; therefore glorify God in your body.

1 Corinthians 6:19–20

Keep Your Body Physically Active

America is a land of conveniences, and therefore our level of physical activity has drastically diminished in the past fifty years. We sit all day at home, school, and work and in the transportation that takes us there. We buy or quickly microwave prepared food. We sit for our recreation—TV, movies, computer games, reading, concerts, or sports events. We don't get up for much—the pizza is delivered, and soon robots will bring the beer and pretzels. We don't even have to get up to shop anymore; we can do it online or on TV. Our sedentary behavior is having a significant impact on our health—our weight, our strength, our flexibility, our balance, and our bodily functions.

Why is physical activity important? Because being moderately physically active improves health by

- helping to build and maintain healthy bones, muscles, and joints
- helping people achieve and maintain a healthy body weight

- increasing feelings of well-being and reducing stress
- reducing feelings of depression and anxiety
- helping older adults become stronger and better able to move about without falling or becoming excessively fatigued

And being physically active reduces premature death by

- lowering the risk of developing high blood pressure, diabetes, and colon cancer
- lowering the risk of dying from heart disease or having a second heart attack
- lowering both cholesterol and triglycerides and increasing "good" cholesterol
- reducing blood pressure in people who have high blood pressure

What can you do to increase your physical activity? Make activity a daily part of your life. Make it enjoyable and work with family members or partners. Set specific goals; start slowly and build up to increasing levels of activity. Try to be active for at least thirty minutes a day on a regular basis.

Here are some tips to get moving:[1]

- Walk, cycle, jog, skate, etc., to work, school, the store, or church.
- Park the car farther away from your destination.
- Get on or off the bus several blocks away from your destination.
- Take the stairs instead of the elevator or escalator.
- Walk the dog.
- Play with the kids.
- Take fitness breaks—walking or doing desk exercises— instead of taking cigarette or coffee breaks.
- Perform gardening or home repair activities.
- Avoid labor-saving devices.
- Use leg power—take small trips.
- Exercise while watching TV.

Not all of us were born with perfect physical temples; we all have weaknesses or vulnerabilities, and some of us have been born with or have acquired physical limitations that affect how we live. Imperfect bodies are still mysterious and miraculous— breathing, pumping blood, maintaining temperature, moving smoothly and reactively, balancing, digesting, detoxifying, and healing. Scientists and physicians continue to learn about and understand the complexity of our wondrous bodies. If we maintain our cars with regular visits to the shop or loving and attentive care, is it not important to give similar attention to our bodies?

Feed Your Body Healthy Food

> God said, "See, I have given you every plant yielding seed
> that is upon the face of all the earth, and every tree with
> seed in its fruit; you shall have them for food."
>
> Genesis 1:29–30

Food is the fuel that keeps your body active and healthy. Your body needs food first thing in the morning and every three to four hours during your active day. That means three meals a day plus one or two healthy snacks. Women need about 2,200 calories of food on an average day, men need 2,800 calories, and children require 1,300 to 2,000 calories per day. Aging and activity levels impact your body's need for fuel. For example, aging decreases your need for fuel. Women age fifty or older need about 1,900 calories, and men over fifty need 2,300 calories. The value of the nutrition in those calories is vitally important. We need calcium to build and maintain strong bones. We need water to keep our cells functioning properly along with fiber to detoxify our digestive system and keep it healthy. We need protein to keep our muscles and organs healthy and strong, and we need healthy fats for our brains and our heart.

Unfortunately, our busy lives and the demand for convenience foods have had a negative impact on our health. We no longer take the time to shop frequently and buy healthy foods, to plan healthy meals in advance, to prepare and cook healthy meals, and to have healthy snacks available. We buy processed foods that are ready to eat or quick to prepare, and we buy fast foods and often eat on the run. The staples of previous generations—fresh fruits and vegetables, whole grains, and fish or lean meats have been replaced by bread, bagels, burgers on buns, fried foods, sugar cereals, and sugar soda pop, pizza, and packaged pasta-based quick meals or soups.

Americans were brought up on the "food pyramid." On average, adults should have 2 to 3 servings daily of dairy products, 2 to 3 servings of meat or other protein sources, 3 to 5 servings of vegetables, 2 to 4 servings of fruits, and 6 to 11 servings of grains such as bread, rice, cereal, and pasta.

Americans are overweight because of too much food and too little activity. One of the current problems is a misunderstanding of what makes up a serving. Serving sizes are defined by the Food Guide Pyramid[2] as follows: 1 serving includes 1 slice of bread, 1 cup of ready-to-eat cereal, or ½ cup of cooked cereal, pasta, or rice; ½ cup of cooked vegetables, 1 cup of raw leafy vegetables, or ¾ cup vegetable juice; 1 medium sized apple, banana, orange, or pear, ½ cup chopped, cooked, or canned fruit, or ¾ cup fruit juice; 1 cup of milk or yogurt, 1½ ounces of natural cheese, or 2 ounces of processed cheese; 2 to 3 ounces of meat, poultry, or fish. The following may be substituted for 1 ounce of meat: ½ cup of cooked dry beans or tofu, 2½ ounces of soyburger, 1 egg, 2 tablespoons of peanut butter, or ⅓ cup of nuts.

Portion sizes of American food are a significant part of the obesity problem. A recent estimate is that American restaurants serve on average 3,800 calories of food per person per day. That is nearly twice what we need to stay healthy (hopefully we are not eating every meal in a restaurant or fast-food outlet). We cannot afford to "supersize" our meals. Examples of the equivalent serving sizes for our common foods include:

- hamburger roll—2 servings
- doughnut—2 servings
- 1 bagel (4½ inch diameter)—4 servings
- 4 pancakes (5 inches in diameter)—6 servings
- croissant—2 servings
- pie—2 servings
- individual bag tortilla chips—2 servings
- movie-style medium box of popcorn—8 servings (the fat equivalent of a bacon and eggs breakfast, hamburger and fries lunch, and a steak and fixings dinner combined)
- 1 medium order french fries—4 servings
- 13-ounce trimmed cooked prime rib—5 servings

As you can see, we consume many more servings of food than the recommendation for staying healthy. One suggestion is to use a smaller plate and not go back for seconds. In a restaurant, order soup or salad and share an entrée. And never supersize unless you are sharing with at least one other person.

Remember that food prepared with added sugar or with fat adds significant calories. For example:

- One baked potato has 120 calories and almost no fat, while 14 french fries have 225 calories and 11 grams of fat.
- One slice of frosted cake or pie has 6 added teaspoons of sugar; an 8-ounce low-fat fruit yogurt has 7; a 10-ounce chocolate shake has 9; a 12-ounce cola has 9; and a 12-ounce fruit drink (not pure fruit juice) has 12.

A diet consisting of a variety of foods is encouraged to assure getting appropriate amounts of the nutrients needed to keep you healthy. One simple way to help with this variety is to be sure that you eat foods of different colors. A new food pyramid has been suggested by Dr. Walter Willett of the Harvard School

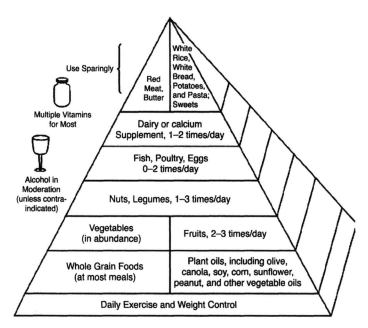

Revision of food pyramid by Dr. Walter C. Willett, from *Eat, Drink, and Be Healthy* (used by permission).

of Public Health as a guide to getting the right balance of healthy nutrients.[3]

Vitamins or Dietary Supplements

It is better that healthy people get their nutrition from a balanced variety of foods (preferably fresh foods) rather than from supplements. Some groups, however, may benefit from a multiple vitamin, especially women who may need extra calcium or iron and teenagers who may not be eating a balanced diet. Vegetarians who do not eat animal products are advised to take a multiple vitamin with iron to address possible iron and vitamin B12 deficiency. People who avoid entire food groups because of allergies or diseases affecting digestion and people who smoke or abuse alcohol may also need vitamin supplements.

Weight

The current measure of appropriate weight for height is the Body Mass Index (BMI). The recommended BMI is between 18.5 and 25. A BMI of 25 to 30 is considered overweight, and 30 and above is obese.

- One method of calculating your BMI is to divide your weight in pounds by your height in inches, and then divide the result by your height in inches, and multiply by 703.
- Another way of assessing your risk related to weight is to measure your waist circumference. If you measure just above your hips, the recommended measurement for women is 35 inches or less, and for men, 40 inches or less.

While achieving and maintaining a healthy weight is an important factor in being healthy, being physically active at any weight is extremely important. Increasing physical activity from your current level of activity has the benefit of increasing energy, improving mood, increasing strength and flexibility, and focusing your mind as well as maintaining or decreasing your weight.

Give Your Body Adequate Rest

> *You have put gladness in my heart*
> *more than when their grain and wine abound.*
> *I will both lie down and sleep in peace;*
> *for you alone, O LORD, make me lie down in safety.*
>
> Psalm 4:7–8

Sleep is as necessary to living a healthy life as food, water, and air. It is frequently not on our priority list and is easily put off for more important things—work, fun, chores, or even television. While the amount of sleep needed by individuals varies, there are general recommendations.[4] Most adults need 7 to 8 hours of sleep per night, teenagers need 9 hours, and infants need 16 hours per day on average. People tend to sleep more lightly and for shorter time spans as they age, although they continue to need the same amount of sleep. Health problems may also impact your sleep patterns.

Getting too little sleep results in a sleep deficit. Our bodies naturally respond to that deficit with sleepiness, which is a signal to get more sleep. While many think they may be getting by with less sleep, this sleep deficit has an impact on our judgment, reaction time, and alertness. If you feel drowsy during the day, you haven't had enough sleep. If you fall asleep within 5 minutes of lying down, you have a sleep deficit. The American cultural practice of "burning the candle at both ends" has resulted in a sleep-deprived population in which drowsiness has become normal. Sleep problems can affect your health, including increasing your risk for motor vehicle accidents and your risk for heart disease.

Our typical hectic and stimulating daily environment is not conducive to rest or getting to sleep. Our work ethic and/or overly full plate spill over and impact our need for rest. The end of the day is for winding down and relaxing. It is not helpful to catch up on emails or professional reading or surf the Internet. It is not restful to start to clean, do laundry, or organize at the end of the day. Going over the demands of the following day should be done earlier. Listening to energizing music or watching stimulating television keep you from relaxing your body and mind or from spending valuable time reading your children to sleep or relaxing with a loved one.

Suggestions to improve your sleep habits include setting a regular bedtime and waking time; relaxing before you go to bed; exercising regularly; avoiding caffeine, alcohol, and tobacco—especially late in the day; and creating a comfortable environment for sleeping without distractions. If you are having significant sleeping problems or daytime drowsiness, discuss it with your doctor.

Naps are beneficial for some individuals, boosting alertness and performance. Guidelines for napping to preserve good nighttime sleep include napping no longer than 45 minutes, allowing 15 minutes to wake up following a nap, and not napping too close to bedtime.

In his book *Sabbath: Finding Rest, Renewal, and Delight in Our Busy Lives* Wayne Muller writes, "Our culture invariably supposes that action and accomplishment are better than rest, that doing something—anything—is better than doing nothing. Because of our desire to succeed, to meet these ever-growing expectations, we do not rest. Because we do not rest, we lose our way."[5] You only cheat yourself when you skimp on rest. The time you think you have by sleeping less is time that you are less effective and less creative. The time you think you are saving may be time lost to the hazards of driving while sleepy or to the health effects of lack of sleep. People who sleep 7 to 8 hours live longer than those who sleep less than 7 or more than 8 hours. Sleep deprivation appears to increase the risk of alcohol and drug abuse and may increase the risk of heart disease.

We know that Jesus slept. According to Luke 8:22–25:

> One day he got into a boat with his disciples, and he said to them, "Let us go across to the other side of the lake." So they put out, and while they were sailing he fell asleep. A windstorm swept down on the lake, and the boat was filling with water, and they were in danger. They went to him and woke him up, shouting, "Master, Master, we are perishing!" And he woke up and rebuked the wind and the raging waves; they ceased, and there was a calm. He said to them, "Where is your faith?"

Jesus was tired from teaching and preaching and went to the back of the boat to find rest. In spite of the storm around him, he remained asleep from fatigue and surrounded by the trust and faith he had in God.

Jesus knew the importance of rest and renewal.

> The apostles gathered around Jesus, and told him all that they had done and taught. He said to them, "Come away to

a deserted place all by yourselves and rest a while." For many were coming and going, and they had no leisure even to eat. And they went away in the boat to a deserted place by themselves. (Mark 6:30–32)

Have a Healthy Sex Life

How beautiful you are, my love,
    how very beautiful!
Your eyes are doves
    behind your veil.
Your hair is like a flock of goats,
    moving down the slopes of Gilead.
Your teeth are like a flock of shorn ewes
    that have come up from the washing,
all of which bear twins,
    and not one among them is bereaved.
Your lips are like a crimson thread,
    and your mouth is lovely.
Your cheeks are like halves of a pomegranate
    behind your veil.
Your neck is like the tower of David,
    built in courses;
on it hang a thousand bucklers,
    all of them shields of warriors.
Your two breasts are like two fawns,
    twins of a gazelle,
    that feed among the lilies.
Until the day breathes
    and the shadows flee,
I will hasten to the mountain of myrrh
    and the hill of frankincense.
You are altogether beautiful, my love;
    there is no flaw in you.

Song of Solomon 4:1–7

What is sex if not a gift from God? Who created our miraculous bodies in all their complexity—from our hair to our toenails, our skin to our blood vessels? Who would imagine the totality of response to someone we love intimately? Who would understand the depth of the closeness and communication that comes from physical oneness? Our bodies were created with the physical, emotional, psychological, relational, and spiritual capacity for sexual love.

Rabbi and spiritual counselor Shoni Labowitz writes in *God, Sex, and Women of the Bible:* "Eve and Adam can guide us in a most sacred way of loving each other and uniting with God. Our journey toward creating a meaningful sacred union starts with Adam *knowing* Eve. . . . In Hebrew, *daat,* the word 'to know,' implies an intimate knowledge of one's self and another, as intimate as lovemaking. . . . When the Bible states that 'Adam *knew* Eve' (Genesis 4:1), it means they made love and birthed new life."[6]

What is sexual health? According to research on adolescent health, sexual health includes the following:[7]

- appreciation of one's own body
- development and maintenance of meaningful interpersonal relationships
- avoidance of exploitative or manipulative relationships
- affirmation of one's own sexual orientation and respect for the sexual orientation of others
- interaction with both genders in respectful and appropriate ways
- expression of affection, love, and intimacy in accord with personal values
- expression of one's sexuality while respecting the rights of others

We cannot deny the reality that we are created by God as sexual beings and that, as such, we need to have healthy outlets for sexual feelings. They can be intentionally directed toward appropriate and positive outlets. Repressed or denied, however, we run the risk of inappropriate expression. Sex is a gift, but the complexity of that gift carries with it a lot of responsibility. Healthy sex is a powerful expression of a mature and healthy individual, secure in one's own body and with enough self-love to share that love deeply with another. Healthy sex is not exploitative, manipulative, or disrespectful. It is not about power or control but about a mutually responsive expression of the deepest love. It is a powerful emotional tool that when misused can destroy lives but when employed healthfully can result in the deepest spiritual connection and can produce new creations conceived in love.

Unhealthy sex affects health and wholeness. A baby conceived without loving responsibility is exposed to multiple risks. Sexually transmitted diseases can be painful, can make you very sick, may be incurable, can progress to cancer, and can be fatal. Practicing safe sex means being knowledgeable about how diseases are transmitted, being abstinent, and using proper protection and/or having a monogamous relationship.

Unhealthy sex is using the powerful physical and emotional connection of our bodies for purposes other than those intended by God. Using sex as a commodity for sale, as a weapon to injure or kill, as a tool to manipulate or control, or as a drug to produce numbness or euphoria is degrading and misusing God's gift. This is not limited to prostitution, knowingly spreading HIV or AIDs, or stranger rape. It includes violent or forced sex within a relationship, addiction to Internet pornography, sexual gratification with a vulnerable person, and sex as an expression of power or authority. Being sexually unhealthy includes the fear of sex or intimacy that may result from the misuse of sex.

Having a healthy sex life in the context of an intimate relationship is important for physical wellness, emotional wellness, and social-interpersonal wellness. The physical, emotional, and spiritual connection in a committed relationship is healing and healthy. This connection of becoming one flesh is fully experienced when two healthy individuals choose sex as a mutual expression of love and commitment. It is essential to nurture the intimacy of the relationship to reap the benefits of that connection. Just as we are amazed by the miraculous complexity of our bodies, we can be amazed and grateful to God for the gift of sexuality.

Questions

1. Describe your eating patterns. Plan to eat a balance of healthy foods, starting with a healthy breakfast and eating every three to four hours until early evening.

2. Calculate your BMI. Estimate your average daily serving portions of fat, carbohydrates, and protein. Include your beverages and water consumption. Consider adding more fruits and vegetables and cutting out sugars (soda pop, cookies, cake, sweetened coffee drinks, juice drinks) or refined carbohydrates (white foods).

3. Estimate your minutes of planned physical activity in a week. Plan to increase by 30 minutes or to increase the intensity of the activities you are currently doing.

4. Think about your usual day. How could you increase your daily physical activity?

5. Consider the gift of healthy sexuality and how it has impacted your life and relationship. How could your sex life improve?

Emotional Well-Being: A Healthy Mind

Put away from you all bitterness and wrath and anger and wrangling and slander, together with all malice, and be kind to one another, tenderhearted, forgiving one another, as God in Christ has forgiven you.

Ephesians 4:31-32

The U.S. Surgeon General has described mental health as "the successful performance of mental function, resulting in productive activities, fulfilling relationships with other people, and the ability to adapt to change and to cope with adversity. Mental health is indispensable to personal well-being, family and interpersonal relationships, and contribution to community or society."[1]

Just as avoiding risky or toxic behaviors and participating in healthy physical activities are helpful in promoting physical health, avoiding risky behaviors and toxic relationships and regularly releasing healthy emotions promote mental health. Abusing alcohol and drugs is a risk for mental and physical health. Continuing in relationships that revolve around the use of alcohol, drugs, or violence is an unhealthy risk. Stiflng your emotions in stressful situations—acutely or chronically—results in physical symptoms, emotional numbness, or inappropriate outbursts. Participating in social groups or activities that encourage the expression of emotions is healthy. Participating in competitive sports or recreation can be a healthy way to release tension and express emotion. Viewing sporting activities can also be a healthful emotional release. Watching movies or reading books or stories that evoke emotions, performing or attending musical performances, and viewing works of art can all be good for emotional health.

Anger and hostility are emotional reactions directly related to heart disease. We cannot avoid anger completely, but we can learn to control it. The natural response to anger is to fight or run away, but these responses result in problems in a social context in which it is inappropriate to fight and not usually convenient to run away. The physiologic factors that prepare us to fight or run result in disease when the anger is not controlled or released appropriately. When you recognize feelings of anger, you have several options. Rather than taking your anger out on someone, recognize that you are angry and respectfully explain why or seek a way to address the problem that has caused the anger. If communicating your feelings is inappropriate, direct your attention away from what is making you angry and use your energy for healthy physical activity. Sometimes it is necessary to defuse the anger quickly by learning to practice a relaxation exercise that physically calms you and directs your attention toward something more positive.

Laughter has been found to be therapeutic for emotional relief, lessening of pain, and increasing of tolerance for difficult or anxiety-producing situations. Laughter also boosts the immune system to aid in healing. Laughter is produced by a complex series of events in our brains that analyze the humor intellectually and emotionally and produce the physical responses of muscles contracting in the face and body, respiratory changes that produce gasping and noises, and tears. All of these things occur in response to stress and as a method to reduce tension. Laughter also creates connections between people. Once someone starts laughing, it is contagious, and the more people laugh together, the more they bond in that shared experience. Laughter is healthy in many ways.

Recognize Stress and Develop Coping Skills

Stress is inevitable and not always bad. The edge of nervousness before preaching, leading a meeting, or singing can sometimes enhance your performance. The challenge of a lively committee meeting can be invigorating and may lead to growth—personal and congregational. Acute stress, however, is common and is often out of our control. It may be the result of illness or injury, separation or divorce, moving, financial difficulties, death or illness of a family member, or a new call or new job. It may be caused by a car accident, staff turnover, capital campaign or building project, problem at your child's school, or renovation of your home.

Common emotional symptoms of stress include irritability, anger, depression, and anxiety. Common physical symptoms include muscle tension, tension headaches, stomachaches or bowel problems (diarrhea or constipation), high blood pressure, heart palpitations, chest pain, and dizziness.[2] Life-threatening trauma can result in what is called post-traumatic stress disorder with symptoms that affect health chronically. Healthy individuals usually weather stressful incidents with time or help. It is when we are not healthy or when stressful incidents are cumulative that stress causes significant mental health problems.

Sometimes living with problematic relationships at home or at work, or living under chronic financial stress or the stress of discrimination results in one becoming physically and psychologically numbed. This can lead to physical illness and/or mental illness over time. About one in five Americans experiences a mental health disorder in the course of a year.

Coping well is anticipating what you can and planning for the time and support needed to deal with things effectively. It is attending to self-care to maximize your health and wellness and having and using a support network of individuals to give physical and emotional support and advice. It means knowing when and where to seek help in specific situations from your friends, peers, mentors, physicians, or others in your community.

Successful coping is related to realistic optimism—the tendency to anticipate positive outcomes. Pessimism, however, is related to avoidance and social isolation, leading to depression and anxiety.[3] The more knowledgeable you are about your own gifts and challenges, the more aware you are of the challenging issues and demands of your work, your family, and your community. And the more you can maintain a positive personal outlook and a positive social support system, the greater is your opportunity to be healthy and to be a strong and effective leader.

Planning for regular vacation or personal time away is equally important. You need personal time for rest, recharging, and recreation as well as for developing nourishing relationships with family and friends. Maintaining a positive attitude and sense of optimism requires the personal energy to listen actively, think creatively, and plan for the future. Incorporating regular relaxation exercises and stretching exercises into your day will relieve muscular tension that creeps up on you during the day.

Susan: RL's Administrative Assistant

Susan is the administrative assistant at Lord of Life Church, where RL is senior pastor. She has been in that position for twelve years—five of those years before RL was called. We serve on the board of a community clinic together. Mental health is a big issue for the community health center, and one night we were talking about job stress and depression.

"You know, I work for a local Protestant congregation. I sometimes wonder how our pastor stays sane. In fact, I worry about him some days. Usually he has been there when I get there, and he has a committee meeting or some other meeting every night. With Saturday and Sunday services, I don't know how he finds time for himself or his family. Lately he has been coming in later in the morning. I don't know where he finds the time to eat. We sometimes have doughnuts with coffee in the morning or occasionally there will be cake or pie left over from the women's meeting. Good thing McDonald's is just around the corner. Usually he loves chatting with the quilting ladies, but he hasn't even done that lately.

"It's got to be tough. Lately there is always some problem. Often there is someone who comes off the freeway asking for money for gas or food for some emergency. I don't think a week goes by that we don't have a member with a new illness or death in the family or some other crisis. Of course, we have the day care—which is fun and helps with the budget, but there is always some minor problem that needs his attention. We are supposed to meet every week, but something usually interrupts and we get cut short or can't meet. Of course, that often means calls in the evening so we can get the bulletin out.

"I love the church. I wouldn't want to be anywhere else. It seems to me that when Pastor Johnson was here, things were a little calmer. But maybe my memory isn't so good. I love Pastor RL, too, but it sure wouldn't surprise me if he up and left. A person just can't work like that forever, you know."

Welcome Change and Learn How to Adapt

Think about your childhood home. How did you feel when your parents redecorated or renovated it? Were you excited about the change or wistful about losing the familiar? How about when it was sold to another family? Were you pleased that another family could live and grow in that home, or were you disappointed that you would not be able to "go home" and see it as it always was? We are creatures of habit and are typically not welcoming of change.

Our culture, however, continues to undergo change. Thinking back one or two generations, we know of individuals who worked for decades at the same job until retirement. As baby boomers, we were told to expect several job changes in our lifetime, and young people today can also expect several changes of occupation. The speed of change is rapidly increasing, and if we are to be fulfilled and feel that we have accomplished what we have been called to do, we must be able to adapt to change.

That does not necessarily mean that we change as individuals or that our values or the things that we hold to be most important change. But the context of our lives and our work is constantly changing, and we must be prepared to adapt to best understand how we can impact our community positively and most effectively.

Psychologist James Prochaska and his colleagues have studied change and have helped us to understand the concept of readiness to change.[4] If you need to change your own behavior to respond to external change or to address an imbalance in your life, you need to understand the stages of change. First, you must be aware of the possibility of change and have a willingness to contemplate what that change may mean to you. To respond to change or make changes in your behavior, you need information and you need to prepare. Have a plan and seek support. When you are ready, make a commitment and act. Finally, plan for ways to help you maintain your change. This may mean using your support system, planning for appropriate rewards, and planning to evaluate your situation to determine whether the change you have made has been successful.

Learn How to Prevent Depression and to Recognize Its Signs

Depression is common, chronic, and costly. It is one of the leading causes of disease worldwide, and it causes more disability than heart disease or strokes. About 9 percent of Americans are diagnosed with depression, but at least 50 percent of depressed individuals are not recognized as being depressed. Individuals who are depressed are at higher risk for heart disease, worsening of other chronic diseases, and premature death. Risk factors for depression include being female, single, socially isolated, unemployed, poor, and having a history of depression.

Symptoms of depression might include sadness that is sometimes overwhelming, but in others it may not be apparent at all or may show up as unexpected tears. Other symptoms include unusual irritability, frustration, worry, discouragement, loss of interest, poor self-image, and preoccupation with physical symptoms such as pain or stomach problems. Sometimes a depressed person has memory or concentration difficulties.

Some simple questions can predict depression, the most important of which are:[5]

1. Have you been feeling down, depressed, or hopeless?
2. Have you been bothered by having little interest or pleasure in doing things?

If the answer to either question is yes, ask yourself the following:

1. Have you been having difficulty sleeping?
2. Has your appetite changed recently?
3. Are you bothered by feelings of worthlessness or inadequacy?
4. Do you have little interest in sex?

Positive answers to any of these questions indicate increased risk of depression. Anyone who appears to be a possible risk and who answers any of these questions positively should be referred to a physician or counselor for evaluation.

Depression is treatable. The most important step toward relief of depression is to recognize it and seek help. Treatment may mean a few visits to a physician or counselor to work out issues related to a situational depression and to plan for changes to address those issues. It could mean antidepressant medication or other medication and behavioral counseling for a longer period of time. For a very few it means long-term medication to address a chemical imbalance that makes some people more vulnerable to depression.

Work at Being Happy

Happy are those whose greatest desire is to do what God requires: God will satisfy them fully!

Matthew 5:6 (GNT)

Depression is a serious illness and needs professional attention and treatment. Many of us are not depressed, but we do experience changing moods. That is very normal. The key thing is to be aware of your emotions and moods and to be knowledgeable about what makes you happy, sad, or angry. Effectively dealing with anger is particularly important, for when anger builds, it can lead to hostility. Both of these emotions are related to heart disease—and specifically to death from heart disease. Constructive communication is important to defuse anger—either as an attempt to resolve conflict or to understand the nature of the conflict. Physical exercise is a good way to direct the energy that comes from anger or strong emotion into a healthful activity.

Make a habit of regularly doing activities that bring you positive healthy emotions. See funny or thrilling movies, go to the zoo or aquarium or to a sports event, play with children or read to them, play a musical instrument or listen to music, create or view works of art, take your pet for a walk or a romp, and celebrate God's word through worship or meditation. Smiling and laughing is very therapeutic in addition to being good exercise for your face! And tears of joy are a healthy outlet for overflowing emotions.

Greg: Assistant to the Bishop

At one of his appointments shortly after his first visit, RL told me about a conversation he had with the assistant to the bishop in his synod. His name was Greg. Greg and RL had been in seminary together and had kept in touch over the years. They had both recently attended the synod leadership retreat. Greg greeted RL and then said, "What's up, buddy? You don't look so hot." RL admitted he had seen a doctor but that he was mostly tired and trying to get back on track. Greg's response was, "You know, frankly, I'm worried about what I've seen lately. Seems so many of our pastors are struggling. They're worn-out, burned out, stressed out.

I wish we had better resources—we don't even have enough rostered leaders to encourage sabbaticals. It's women and men, all ages, but especially pastors in their forties who have been in ministry for fifteen to twenty years."

He went on to say, "I know times are tough financially, and congregations are struggling with budgets that don't meet needs. I'm sure there are issues with being understaffed and certainly with conflicts over how to make the budget stretch. Even worse, though, I hear pastors talking more about how isolated they feel. They don't feel supported by their peers or by the synod office. I've heard more discussion about being competitive with the other local churches. I don't know what to do about meeting their needs. We're already stretched too thin at the synod office, and it seems we're just trying to put out the fires. It's the church that cries out the loudest that gets the attention, or the pastor who's in major trouble."

RL had listened and had tried to be empathetic, but he told me it was hard to even feign interest because he was too tired to care about anyone's needs but his own.

Questions

1. What makes you laugh? What makes you happy? What regular activity do you do or have you planned that will give you a good hour or two of laughter and happiness?

2. What are your personal signs of stress? What do you do or are you planning to regularly relieve symptoms due to stress? What are you planning to do to remedy the cause of the stress?

3. What change(s) are you experiencing or anticipating in your life? How are you responding to or preparing for this change?

Intellectual Well-Being

My child, if you accept my words
and treasure up my commandments within you,
making your ear attentive to wisdom
and inclining your heart to understanding;
if you indeed cry out for insight,
and raise your voice for understanding;
if you seek it like silver,
and search for it as for hidden treasures—
then you will understand the fear of the LORD
and find the knowledge of God.
For the LORD gives wisdom;
from his mouth come knowledge and understanding;
he stores up sound wisdom for the upright;
he is a shield to those who walk blamelessly,
guarding the paths of justice
and preserving the way of his faithful ones.
Then you will understand righteousness and justice
and equity, every good path.

Proverbs 2:1–9

Exercise Your Mind

A healthy mind is clearly supported and enhanced by a healthy body. Studies have shown that regular physical activity reduces symptoms of anxiety and depression. Just as regular physical activity improves physical health, regular mental activity improves mental health. Studies have shown that mental exercises can help memory and delay symptoms of dementia, and that listening to and learning music enhances thinking. Doing crossword puzzles and mathematical puzzles, learning new skills, practicing a musical instrument, or reading challenging books are good examples of intellectual activities. The key is to make the activity a regular habit.

Learning is not just a solitary activity. At times, it is necessary to work with a teacher or mentor to adequately learn a new skill or topic. At other times, learning in a group enriches the learning experience by adding others' viewpoints and experiences, and it results in creative thinking that would not have been possible alone. Often, learning by reading or listening is not enough; doing is better. While at times we must learn by solitary trial and error, the fastest way to learn is to do an activity under supervision with support and feedback. As professionals, we may be uncomfortable in that role. Nevertheless, there is always opportunity for learning by asking someone you trust and admire to observe and assist you in vocational growth.

Reading or learning outside your vocation or occupation leads to new experiences personally and relationally. Learning new skills builds up new memories and new nerve networks, keeping the brain functioning at an increased capacity. Practice activities or learn new skills that use your nondominant hand. Learning and performing musically is therapeutic emotionally as well as cognitively. Performing in a group is another way to be enriched socially.

Learning often comes as a result of a question. Living life fully—exposed to art, music, sports, politics, science, religions, history—keeps curiosity alive. In medicine we teach about best evidence. To find the best evidence that might change how you practice, it is essential to ask the right question. Does a child with an ear infection recover more quickly with an antibiotic than with fever and pain control with over-the-counter medication?

The intuitive answer would be yes, because that is the way we have practiced for years. With the right studies, however, we have learned that 80 percent of the time children recover from ear infections without antibiotics. The question then becomes, are we doing good or harm by using antibiotics for every ear infection?

Questions aren't just limited to your work. They may be related to hobbies or the world around us. What plants grow in the shade? Who composed that song I just heard on the radio? What is it like to live with paralysis? How have others successfully lost weight? What do Muslims believe? Do children learn more effectively using computers? How do you say, "Happy Birthday!" in Spanish? What is arthritis anyway, and what can I do about it?

"Use it or lose it" applies to the brain as well as the body. New research has shown that those who continue to actively challenge their minds are less at risk for developing Alzheimer's disease. Learning is fun. We are much more likely to learn new things when we avoid the mind- and body-numbing activity of watching television, playing repetitive computer games, or gambling at a casino. Turn it off and read, take a class, visit the library or museum, learn to play an instrument, join a quartet or choir, take up a new sport or recreational activity, travel, or join a Scrabble, chess, or bridge club.

We are more likely to learn and enjoy learning when it is a topic that fascinates us or that we are passionate about. Some people have a childhood fascination that carries them throughout life—music, space travel, mechanics, or animals. Others find a new interest later in life—photography, writing, carpentry, or gardening.

Lifelong Learning

Education has the strongest impact on improving memory and avoiding dementia. The intellectual stimulation that continuing education provides exercises the memory and helps maintain the nerve networks that keep the mind functioning well into old age. In addition, continuing education refreshes your ministry with new ideas and new skills, gives you an opportunity to develop new relationships and a collegial support system, and helps you deal with conflict or change. A sabbatical can do the same when focused on scholarly or professionally related enrichment.

Lifelong learning also revitalizes our lives when we study new ideas, acquire new skills, or improve skills or gifts we already have. Learning about other faiths can help to ground us in our own faith and give us greater understanding of those of different faiths. Taking classes in the arts or in music enhances creativity and helps develop natural gifts or talents. Having a creative outlet is also very therapeutic for stress relief and emotional fulfillment.

Specific experiences or questions may lead you in a particular direction. As a new physician in practice, I had to learn the ropes of the business of medicine early and quickly because I started up a new clinic with one other partner. Everything we did was from scratch and with little mentoring. Learning the hard way was helpful in my own practice and in teaching. What I discovered in teaching, however, was that although I had my own experience to fall back on, it wasn't enough. I went back and took a brief professional course on the business of healthcare. I discovered that I enjoyed learning in that group experience and that it was very helpful in teaching and practice. It ultimately led to a master's degree in business for me. At this point in my life, I don't think more degrees are in the picture, but more learning certainly is. I am eager to have more time for music performance. I would love to take golf lessons or photography classes. I enjoy traveling and learning about new places. I love to go to art galleries—to take in the beauty and creative experience of the art and to learn about the artist. I know from my own experience that lifelong learning keeps me creative and energized in life and in work.

People often ask family physicians, "How can you know enough about everything to see any age patient for any problem?" The answer is that the most common problems present most commonly, and the most important thing to know is what you don't know and what you will then do for the patient to be sure the problem gets addressed. As physicians, we learn every day, and the more we learn, the more we realize we don't know. The more we learn, however, the more we are able to help our patients heal and learn about their own bodies and illnesses or injuries. The biggest danger in medicine is a physician who believes he or she knows everything and is always right. That is when problems arise in medical care and in patient relationships. A wise physician learns to live with uncertainty and to not be afraid of saying, "I don't know. But I will do my best to find out for you."

Martin Luther writes in the Preface to the Large Catechism:

Therefore, I appeal once more to all Christians, especially the pastors and preachers, that they not try to become doctors too soon and imagine that they know everything. (Vain imaginations, like new cloth, suffer shrinkage!) Let all Christians drill themselves in the catechism daily, and constantly put it into practice, guarding themselves with the greatest care and diligence against the poisonous infection of such security or arrogance. Let them constantly read and teach, learn and meditate and ponder. Let them never stop until they have proved by experience and are certain that they have taught the devil to death and have become more learned than God himself and all his saints. If they show such diligence, then I promise them—and their experience will bear me out—that they will gain much fruit and God will make excellent people out of them. Then in due time they will make the noble confession that the longer they work with the catechism, the less they know of it, and the more they have to learn. Only then, hungry and thirsty, will they for the first time truly taste what now they cannot bear to smell because they are so bloated and surfeited. To this end may God grant his grace! Amen.[1]

When you are continuing to grow and learn, you are passionate in your vocation and are perceived by others as inspirational and welcoming to others.

Daughter Deborah

On the fourth visit, I could see a difference in RL. His face was more animated. His shoulders were more squared off, as if a burden had been lightened. I greeted him and he smiled back. I commented on his appearance and speculated that things must be going better. "Well, doc, I had a breakthrough moment. I had a conversation with my daughter last weekend that really made a difference for both of us. You know she has been thinking about being a pastor. I really couldn't get excited about that, and I don't really know why. I've been thinking about it. It's not that she's a woman—I have had really good relationships with my colleagues who are women. It's not about my daughter—she really does have gifts for ministry and seems to be sincere about being a pastor.

"She came to me again this weekend and said, 'Dad, I know you aren't so sure about me going to seminary. I just wanted to tell you how proud I am of you and your love for the church and the people in your congregation. I used to see you up in the pulpit when I was a kid. I thought you looked so big! But more than that, you looked so happy—talking to us as if you were sharing an important secret meant just for each of us individually. I want to feel that way about what I do. I want to share the love of Jesus Christ. Tell me about what it is like to be a pastor.'

"Wow! That was tough. I hadn't thought much about what it's like and wasn't particularly in the mood to answer.

But how could I avoid it? I shook my head, just to get the cobwebs out and try to get to the truth. I looked at her eyes and saw that piercing look from a daughter who really needed to know.

"'I remember the day I was ordained,' I began. 'It was a solemn sacred day and a day of celebration. It was the day that my personal call to ministry was confirmed and supported by my bishop and my peers. It was such a powerful feeling of emotion and responsibility. I felt surrounded by the love and support of my peers and lifted by the love of God. Then I started my first call at First Lutheran. It was a wake-up call. I had to learn everything new—names, faces, places, committees, staff relationships, worship planning, confirmation—never mind being a newlywed! But I loved it. I was involved in the lives of my parishioners—baptisms, weddings, funerals. I truly felt called to serve in that community of faith.'"

"As I went on to tell her about the ups and downs, joys and frustrations of parish ministry, a lightbulb went off for me. I relived the emotions and the significant moments of my own ministry, and in telling her my story, I realized the story was not finished."

This was an important moment for RL, a recommitment to ministry and a special connection with his daughter as they looked forward to the future.

Questions

1. How are you exercising your mind on a regular basis?

2. What new skills would you like to learn? Or what old skills would you like to renew or enhance?

3. Be aware of questions that come to mind. Write them down and seek answers.

Social/Interpersonal Well-Being: High-Quality Personal Relationships

5

The Scriptures focus on the self in relation to God, to community, to the earth. . . . It is not enough for one person to be disease-free. All humans, the whole creation, and the Creator must be in the right relation.

—James P. Wind, *A Letter on Peace and Good Health*[1]

Love God

We love because [God] first loved us.

1 John 4:19

By this we know that we love the children of God, when we love God and obey his commandments.

1 John 5:2

For those of us whose vocation it is to love the children of God and to teach and obey God's commandments, our call is to love because God first loved us. We must bear in mind this unconditional love from God to all his children then love God in return, as a newborn infant responds to the loving care of a parent. This love is critical for our health and wellness, as evidenced by "failure to thrive," a diagnosis for young children who are not healthy and who sometimes die simply because they do not receive loving care. It is most evident in countries where orphanages are so full of children that there are not enough caretakers to give each child physical and emotional attention.

Knowing God's love and returning that love results in an overflowing of love for others and a deep-seated love of self. God's love is the nourishment that keeps us thriving and gives us the energy we need to love our families and our neighbors. When we are secure in God's love, we feel the need to share it. Since the earth and all of its people belong to God, it is right that our love should encompass the earth and its people.

Love Yourself

> *We have been entrusted with a boundless treasure of health-giving and healing riches. Our bodies indeed are temples of the Holy Spirit, and they are to be cared for in ways that recognize just what a marvelous creation each one of us is.*
>
> —James P. Wind, *A Letter on Peace and Good Health*

If we would just treat our bodies, minds, and spirits with the same tender, conscientious care we do our automobiles or our pets, we certainly would be healthier and happier. If we accept the greatest commandment to love the Lord with all our heart, mind, soul, and strength, and to love our neighbors as we love ourselves, this would be unquestioned. Loving yourself means taking care of yourself in all ways—not to the exclusion of others, but because we are loved by God and for the purpose of loving our neighbors.

Self-care is not selfish. We are stewards of our bodies just as we are stewards of other gifts received from God. Self-care means understanding the meaning of positive health and working toward it. Self-care means attending to the balance of the Wholeness Wheel (see page 8). Eat nutritionally and be physically active; take rest, vacation and Sabbath; attend to relationships; learn new information, ideas, and skills; seek vocational feedback and guidance; and tend to personal spiritual needs and spiritual formation.

Self-care means being aware of your physical and emotional needs. Listen to the physical signs of hunger, fatigue, and restlessness. Recognize feelings of sadness, frustration, and anger, and find healthy ways to express those emotions or to encourage positive emotions. Take time to answer questions that arise by seeking out information and knowledge. Listen to the voices around you and try to meet unmet needs of time and attention. Listen to the voice of God around you every day and ask for guidance. Listen to your heart and know that you are using your gifts to make God's world a better place. Parker Palmer, teacher and leader in higher education, writes: "By surviving passages of doubt and depression on the vocational journey, I have become clear about at least one thing: self-care is never a selfish act—it is simply good stewardship of the only gift I have, the gift I was put on earth to offer to others. Anytime we can listen to true self and give it the care it requires, we do so not only for ourselves but for the many others whose lives we touch."[2]

Love Your Family

Husbands should love their wives as they do their own bodies. He who loves his wife loves himself. For no one ever hates his own body, but he nourishes and tenderly cares for it, just as Christ does for the church, because we are members of his body.

Ephesians 5:28–30

And whoever does not provide for relatives, and especially for family members, has denied the faith and is worse than an unbeliever.

1 Timothy 5:8

Many studies have shown the benefits of social relationships to health. Several have shown a decreased risk of early mortality for those involved in social relationships and activities. Others show increased intellectual functioning and emotional health related to being socially active. Still others demonstrate the importance of family support in promoting and improving health and in managing chronic diseases. For adults, marriage is the most influential relationship on health.[3]

Just as you should practice self-care, you also need to care for relationships. Intimate social relationships help us to better understand and love ourselves and to be happy and fulfilled. Through platonic relationships, we are better able to understand others and the world around us. Understanding our family of origin helps us to fully understand ourselves. We need to tend those relationships so that they can help us develop our full potential through their support and guidance. Experiencing intimately the fullness of this life, from birth to death, is important to be able to serve and understand others and effectively address their needs.

Adolescence and young adulthood is the time when we are socialized to seek out special intimate relationships beyond our family of origin. Finding that special relationship and growing into love and living together take up a lot of energy and time for young adults. After time has passed, our attention is directed toward work and/or raising children. If we are single, we often give too much of ourselves to our work. We often lose that special feeling of closeness that is a precious memory from the beginning of a romantic relationship or a special friendship. We get lost in the expectations of work and career and in the constant demands of daily life—especially daily life with children. Because we are focused on the daily grind, we lose touch with friends and family who were so important to us in our young adult lives.

Intimate relationships will sustain a spark of life for a long time but will inevitably cool without attention. Planning for regular time to renew a friendship or romance and to maintain that connection is necessary to assure the kind of support and advocacy, total acceptance and comfort that intimate relationships provide. Having the knowledge that you are loved and cherished by others and that they are available for you when you are in need is an important security measure that sustains you through difficult times or the demands of daily life. Having a network of loving friends and family is very important protection and prevention from falling into or being stuck in unhealthy relationships.

Having children is a very special gift from God and is the opportunity to experience the miraculous. Author and rabbi Shoni Labowitz writes about this emotional time: "Parents at the moment of conception open a channel for something new to take place in this world. The hopes and dreams they plant in the newborn together, they also plant within each other, creating a new level of optimism."[4] This great wonderment and expectation are the joy and the burden of parenting. The love that one feels for a child is immeasurable, and the need to protect that child out of overwhelming love is in tension with letting go. The expectation for the life and vocation of that child is in tension with a child's individuality and independence. Labowitz comments on the parents' relationship: "If all their energies are focused only on the newborn baby, then they are missing out on the mystery."[5] She goes on to talk about the importance of those who participated in the creation of the child—God, the mother, and the father. A child needs love, support, and direction within the context of growing relationships and the continuing love of the parents and God.

Mother Theresa once said, "Just allow people to see Jesus in you—to see how you pray, to see how you lead a pure life, to see how you deal with your family, to see how much peace there is in your family. Then you can look straight into their eyes and say, 'This is the way.' You speak from life, you speak from experience."[6]

Love Your Neighbors

Do not withhold good from those to whom it is due,
when it is in your power to do it.
Do not say to your neighbor, "Go, and come again,
tomorrow I will give it"—when you have it with you.
Do not plan harm against your neighbor
who lives trustingly beside you.
Do not quarrel with anyone without cause,
when no harm has been done to you.
Do not envy the violent
and do not choose any of their ways;
for the perverse are an abomination to the LORD,
but the upright are in his confidence.

Proverbs 3:27–32

I give you a new commandment, that you love one another.
Just as I have loved you, you also should love one another.
By this everyone will know that you are my disciples, if you
have love for one another.

John 13:34–35

When we are successfully caring for ourselves and our closest relationships, we are fully able to care for others. We need to have the skills to build and maintain appropriate relationships with coworkers and staff and with congregation members or those we serve. We need to be able to listen and to try to understand others' experiences or points of view. We need to be able to communicate with words, actions, and attitudes that will be received and understood. We need to be able to work effectively in teams and understand the work of our teams in the context of the congregation or community.

External relationships are essential for being fulfilled vocationally. Professional or work-related relationships are important for personal growth through collegial sharing or professional mentoring. Working successfully in teams—whether a professional team, such as a church staff, or social team, such as a quilting group—teaches social and other skills that enable us to be of greater service to our communities than we could be as individuals. Reaching out to others expands our understanding of different experiences and different cultures. It is only through these relationships that we can be aware of injustices or of other perspectives that can both challenge and enrich our lives.

Church staffs do not necessarily function well naturally as teams. The development of a well-functioning team requires understanding each person's gifts and styles, communicating well with each other, consensus on mission and how to accomplish the work, and taking time for support and fun. If you are experiencing stress or dysfunction within your ministry team, seek professional help. It is as important for the health of the church as it is for your personal health to ask for guidance, input, and remedies toward healthy teamwork. That help may be available to you through the church or through private counseling or coaching services.

Did you know that volunteering is good for your health? In *Purpose and Power in Retirement,* Harold G. Koenig, the well-known geriatrician writes of several healthy outcomes:

- Volunteering is associated with better mental health, increased levels of life satisfaction and self-esteem, greater social networks, and more altruistic behavior.
- Volunteering has been shown to be a source of enhanced career development.
- Any level of volunteering decreases mortality significantly for those who attend religious services frequently.[7]

Opportunities to volunteer are everywhere—from simple random acts of kindness every day, to helping to build homes for others, to acting as a big brother or sister to a child in need of a mentor. The greatest health benefit comes from volunteer acts that are face-to-face, whether you are serving food at a homeless shelter or providing loving arms to infants or children who are hurting.

Although direct service is healthful, it cannot meet the tremendous needs of our community and our world. Kent Groff, a pastor and spiritual director, writes of Samaritan stewardship that is direct and indirect.[8] He includes some other examples of intercession or loving by proxy:

- Service becomes prayer. Actions such as voting, writing legislative representatives, supporting agencies that serve those in need, walking for hunger and other needs, volunteering time and expertise on boards of charitable organizations, are indirect ways of service, and they can be intercessory prayer when approached prayerfully. Authentic service by proxy needs to be grounded by some hands-on or face-to-face service.
- Prayer becomes service. We simply cannot be everywhere or give to every cause or do every act personally. Let each breath serve as a positive arrow of compassion instead of a negative feeling of guilt.

Giving back speaks of grace; it is our debt of gratitude.

Mutual Ministry

I was making a presentation at a congregational conference on health and wellness. At the end of the presentation, Carol, the chair of a congregation's mutual ministry committee, came up to speak with me. She thanked me for the presentation and then launched into her comments. "This is so important. I have seen pastor after pastor start with excitement and enthusiasm. When I was young, my pastor was a role model for me. My family didn't go to church, but my friends told me about the fun they were having in their church's youth program. I visited one day, loved it, and started going regularly. My pastor was full of life. He knew how to connect with us, spoke our language, and welcomed us by creating a comfortable and fun place to learn about life and faith. I joined that congregation as a young adult and attended there for years. Over time I saw my pastor lose his passion, struggle with a congregation in conflict, and finally leave. I heard he was treated for depression, and I don't know if he is in another parish. We had an interim pastor and really worked hard on mission and vision and called a new pastor. Unfortunately, the conflict had not been resolved, and the new pastor got caught up in the issue—clearly supporting one side. Sadly, he left abruptly because of sexual misconduct. It was so clear to me at that time that it is hard for a pastor to be healthy, especially in a congregation that is also unhealthy.

"Since that time, I have been involved in congregational committee work. This is the first time I have been on a mutual ministry committee. I really feel that this committee has made a big difference in the health of our current pastor and the health of our congregation. I could see the same thing happening again to our pastor. We reached out to him at a recent committee meeting. For the first time, we began to talk about health and teamwork and the relationship of healthy church staff and a healthy congregation. We recognized situations that were barriers to maintaining the health of our pastor and staff. We recognized and supported the pastor's need for two days off a week. We set limits for the frequency of evening meetings. We encouraged him to plan for a sabbatical in the next year. I know it is just a start, but I can already see the difference in his mood and energy level. I feel so gratified and relieved to be able to try to prevent a repeat situation that doesn't do our pastor or our congregation any good."

Questions

1. How do you keep a living relationship with God?

2. How do you show love for yourself in your daily life?

3. Who is most important in your life? How are you maintaining healthy relationships?

4. How do you seek out new relationships?

5. How are you expressing love for your community?

Vocational Well-Being 6

> *I exhort the elders among you to tend the flock of God that is in your charge, exercising the oversight, not under compulsion but willingly, as God would have you do it—not for sordid gain but eagerly. Do not lord it over those in your charge, but be examples to the flock. And when the chief shepherd appears, you will win the crown of glory that never fades away.*
>
> 1 Peter 5:1–4

Seek Fulfillment in Your Vocation

Parker J. Palmer writes in his book *Let Your Life Speak: Listening for the Voice of Vocation*, "Vocation does not come from willfulness. It comes from listening."[1] We are often too busy planning and living our lives to stop and listen to who we are and how we must live. Too often childhood experiences lead to jobs, technical training, or college majors and eventually to occupations with little thought about what is truly important or meaningful. Palmer writes, "It takes time and hard experience . . . to sense that running beneath the surface of the experience I call my life, there is a deeper and truer life waiting to be acknowledged."[2]

One definition of fulfillment is to develop the full potentialities of your vocation. To achieve that sense of fulfillment is to understand your personal potential and how that potential can best be used to achieve personal happiness and to respond to God's call. Palmer writes, "Before I can tell my life what I want to do with it, I must listen to my life telling me who I am. I must listen for the truths and values at the heart of my own identity, not the standards by which I must live—but the standards by which I cannot help but live if I am living my own life."[3] To hear the call or find fulfillment involves taking time for personal evaluation and time to listen to your own thoughts and the thoughts of others. Being creative and considering taking healthy risks require energy. Finding true vocation is often enhanced through education or mentoring. Just because you have completed a "terminal" degree program doesn't mean the learning is over. Just because you have been ordained doesn't mean that parish ministry is the only ministry to which you have been called. Seeking true vocation as an adult can sometimes be accomplished only through an intentionally planned sabbatical that takes you out of your daily life and frees your mind to stretch beyond the four walls of everyday demands.

Be Confident in Your Calling

> *My child, do not let these escape from your sight:*
>   *keep sound wisdom and prudence,*
> *and they will be life for your soul*
>   *and adornment for your neck.*
> *Then you will walk on your way securely*
>   *and your foot will not stumble.*
> *If you sit down, you will not be afraid;*
>   *when you lie down, your sleep will be sweet.*
> *Do not be afraid of sudden panic,*
>   *or of the storm that strikes the wicked;*
> *for the LORD will be your confidence*
>   *and will keep your foot from being caught.*

Proverbs 3:21–26

Confidence comes from knowing yourself, including your gifts and talents, and from having developed skills through education and training that make the most of those gifts and talents. We are learning new things from the time of our birth until our final days. One of our biggest challenges is to recognize our own gifts and talents and to acknowledge our weaknesses and dislikes. We will be most confident in our calling and consequently have the greatest positive impact on those around us when we find the work we most enjoy and the community in which we can do it.

Self-confidence is not as easy when our Wholeness Wheel is out of balance. Fatigue, excess weight, or loneliness drains the energy needed to build confidence. Self-confidence is a result of the right "fit" of gifts to service and of "fitness" to trust that one is able to make the most of the gifts God has given.

Leave a Legacy

Reading obituaries is something most of us do by a certain age. Others find themselves doing it at an early age because of occupational roles or because of the closeness of their community. The purpose of a well-written obituary is to distill into a few well-chosen words the meaning of an individual's life and to create a vivid picture of that person. The most memorable obituaries accomplish that goal, not by listing the titles and awards given during a person's life, but by describing that person's passion in life and the impact he or she had on community or family.

If we live our lives from the perspective of future generations, we are more likely to make decisions for the long-term. This might involve asking, "What does this mean?" each time we need to make a decision. Whether we are considering issues of education, jobs, vocation, family, retirement, or location, asking, "What does this mean?" helps us to make meaningful choices.

Manage Time Well

Managing time means being proactive and planning. Knowing the predictable events in your calendar and leaving flexibility for those unpredictable but not unexpected events is the key. Knowing your own rhythms is essential—when you have the most energy and/or the most focus and when you need to get away or get rest to refocus and reenergize. Find the right tools to help organize your time and your work. Develop a team approach to managing tasks, whether at work or at home. When each member of the team knows his or her responsibility and has the opportunity to work toward a common goal, more can be accomplished with less wasted energy.

Schedule specific time for balancing your Wholeness Wheel. Include regular physical activities and time for healthy food, friends and family, rest and renewal, worship and prayer, and fun. Keep in mind your daily, weekly, monthly, and yearly calendar. Sabbaticals don't just happen; they require significant planning in advance.

Understand the Purpose of Work

Americans tend to be workaholics. Workaholics don't work to live; they live to work. Their goal is more money, more things, or more prestige. They work at the expense of all the other areas of life that must be in balance to be healthy. Joan Chittister writes about living the rule of St. Benedict today with respect to the spirituality of work in the world.[4] Work is your gift to the world—your social fruitfulness. Work is the way you are saved from total self-centeredness. It gives you a reason to exist that is larger than yourself and gives hope. Work leads to self-fulfillment, using the gifts and talents you know you have; and it calls on gifts of which you are unaware.

In our culture, we are defined by our work. When introducing ourselves, we give our name and then our occupation or profession. Some struggle with introductions when they work at home to support their families or when their jobs are not defined by a title. Others announce titles that have little meaning to the listeners.

Work is what you do, not who you are. The closer your work matches who you are, however, the healthier you will be. Having a true sense of purpose in life and a sense of mastery of life's challenges using the gifts you have been given leads to positive health.

Grow in Your Profession

Lifelong learning is the key to personal and professional growth. Sometimes lifelong learning is specific to improving skills you need for your work, such as conflict management or counseling. And sometimes it is necessary for your personal growth or for creativity and innovation in your work to learn something that has less relation to your profession. Maybe you have always wanted to take voice lessons or to refresh your learning on a musical instrument. Maybe photography is your hobby and you would like to be more creative and directed in your personal photography. Being intentional about expanding your experience and knowledge gives self-confidence and renewed passion for life. Perhaps taking photography allows you to see things from different perspectives than you have in the past. Confidence in your musical abilities allows you to express yourself, to connect with others emotionally, and to share the gift of music with others.

We witness growth all around us, in young children and in nature. Growth requires essential ingredients that are turned into energy that feeds the growth process. Among those essential ingredients are oxygen, sunlight, water, food or nutrients, and movement. Animals also need emotional nurturing and modeling of mature behavior. The ingredients for professional growth, on the other hand, are learning and practice. Professional growth is enhanced by nurturing relationships, expending creative energy, modeling mentors, stretching for goals, being responsive to change, and learning from failure.

Update on RL

It had been six months since I had first seen RL. He had come on this day to have his blood pressure rechecked. He had been on two medications and had required some dosage adjustment. He never had needed antidepressant medication, although we had discussed it seriously on more than one visit. He was continuing to see a pastoral counselor for personal counseling and also for ministry and leadership coaching. He had been diligent with his homework, and I could see progress at each visit.

"I'm just thrilled to see that you have lost twelve pounds," I told RL. "I know it has been a struggle, but I also know that you are really making a difference in your health," I said.

"I feel so much better. I have more energy and more interest in life. Some of it is the weight loss, but I am sleeping better and eating better too. I'm embarrassed but thrilled to tell you my sex life has really improved! And I actually look forward to going into church in the morning—well, most mornings. I have been able to work out a plan to almost always get two days off a week. I have a list of pastors available to help me out and have been able to build a better system of help with congregational members. It has really made a difference. I hope to have a three-month sabbatical next fall, and the congregation is really working on reaching out to the community to encourage new members and also to meet the needs of the community as we can."

"You look like a new man!" I exclaimed. "Did you think about this as a possibility when you came in six months ago?"

He laughed, "Well, I actually was dragging myself in here

just to satisfy my wife. I didn't really expect much—I didn't really have much hope that things could be different. I know I still have a way to go, but now I know it's possible. I had to change my lifestyle. It's been hard, and I still have changes to make, but I can do it now. My family is very supportive and has been helpful. Sarah is cooking differently, and my sons join me regularly for one-on-one basketball. Sarah and I go for a walk almost every day. I really look forward to that time together—we have some great talks on those walks."

"I'm impressed," I said. "I think you're doing great. Your blood pressure is under control. You've made changes that have made a significant difference in your health. I don't think you need to come back to see me for three months. What's your plan between now and then?"

"I hope to lose another four or five pounds," RL replied. "I plan on increasing the distance that we're walking. I'm looking forward to a theological conference next month— it's on a topic that I'm really interested in. I'm going with another pastor friend. She and I have been meeting regularly with a few other pastors to share ideas and to do text study. I sure appreciate the support you've given me. I'm at a much different place than when we first met."

Questions

1. How/when/where are (were) you most fulfilled in your vocation?

2. On a scale of 1 (outstanding) to 5 (pathetic)—rate your self-confidence. Why did you choose that rating? How does that impact your vocation?

3. Write a brief obituary or a legacy for friends and family, centering on what you most want others to know about your life.

4. Where do you need (would you like) to grow in your profession?

Spiritual Well-Being

My child, do not forget my teaching,
but let your heart keep my commandments;
for length of days and years of life
and abundant welfare they will give you.
Do not let loyalty and faithfulness forsake you;
bind them around your neck,
write them on the tablet of your heart.
So you will find favor and good repute
in the sight of God and of people.
Trust in the LORD with all your heart,
and do not rely on your own insight.
In all your ways acknowledge him,
and he will make straight your paths.

Proverbs 3:1–6

Remember the Wholeness Wheel, in which spiritual health surrounds and supports you and all other dimensions of your health? It is not just a pretty picture; evidence supports it. Harold G. Koenig lists several groundbreaking findings from the Duke Center for the Study of Religion/Spirituality and Health:

1. People who regularly attend church, pray individually, and read the Bible have significantly lower blood pressure than the less religious.
2. People who attend church regularly are hospitalized much less often than people who never or rarely participate in religious services.

3. People with strong religious faith are less likely to suffer depression from stressful life events and more likely to recover from depression.

4. The deeper a person's religious faith, the less likely he or she is to be crippled by depression related to hospitalization for illness.

5. People with strong faith who suffer from physical illness have significantly better health outcomes than less religious people.

6. People who attend religious services regularly have stronger immune systems.

7. Religious people are physically healthier into later life and live longer. Religious faith appears to protect the elderly from heart disease and cancer.[1]

To some, these findings may be surprising. To others, being connected to the God who made us in all our complexity and living out that connection daily is obviously directly related to health. From the Wholeness Wheel perspective, having a full and deep spiritual life gives us the incentive and strength to keep all other dimensions of health in balance.

Why then are church leaders suffering poorer health than in previous decades? Why is there more heart disease and depression? It could be that faith is taken for granted. The very reason individuals discerned a call to public ministry and to be educated and trained for that ministry has taken a backseat to the daily demands of being the leader of a congregation. In the face of overwhelming expectations from congregation members dealing with their own personal imbalances, your own wholeness and particularly your own spiritual wellness may have been left behind.

Be Knowledgeable about Your Faith

Read the Bible regularly, join a study group, take classes, and/or go to seminars to learn more about faith traditions or issues of faith in the community and the world. Ask questions of others about their understanding of faith or faith practices. Seek a mentor in your pastor, a spiritual director, or a theologian. Talk with your family about your faith heritage or their faith journeys. Write regularly in a journal about your spiritual journey. Talk with God and with others about doubts or challenges to faithfulness.

Seek spiritual direction. In *Living Day by Day,* Debra Farrington writes, "Trying to explore the depths of our relationship with God alone is akin to wandering in the forest solo. Even if you know your destination, you will find it hard to find your way without paths and markers on the journey."[2] She describes spiritual direction as the process of two people watching for God's presence in their life together. It is easy to become distracted from your relationship with God because of the busyness of everyday life, the demands on your attention from family and parish, and your own sense of importance or direction.

Make a habit of lifelong learning in theology and ministry. Use the money that is provided by your congregation for that purpose, or if it is not available, explain the essential importance of investing in your spiritual health. Return periodically to your seminary to gather with your friends and peers in renewing your faith and awakening the hunger for knowledge you had as a student.

Practice Your Faith

> *Train yourself in godliness, for, while physical training is of some value, godliness is valuable in every way, holding promise for both the present life and the life to come.*
>
> 1 Timothy 4:7–8

Practicing healthy behaviors such as physical activity, nutritional eating, and restful sleep may be easier than working on spiritual health. Balancing the dimensions of health in your life, especially faith hardiness, requires intentional spiritual habits. Establish a daily prayer time or ritual to keep your conversation with God alive and meaningful. Journal about your own faith or record your reflections on Bible passages or other sacred or theological writings. Make a plan to read and reread the Bible in its entirety. Many faithful Christians have not read the Bible from beginning to end, but for those who have, rereading the Scriptures can shed new light on familiar words.

Remember that there is value in combining activities. A simple example is praying before a meal, thanking God for nutritional foods that keep our bodies fit for service and full of energy. Some find special meaning in prayer walking, often praying for people, situations, the environment, or the community that is a part of the walk. Labyrinths can be a resource to help people focus their minds and hearts in prayer. Relaxation exercises can be done with a favorite Bible verse. Rather than turning on the TV while doing your time on the stationary bicycle, have a conversation with God or sing or listen to your favorite hymns. Find time for regular devotion or study, both alone and in groups. Find a corporate worship setting that helps you grow in your faith and in community with others and attend regularly.

Practice forgiveness. L. Gregory Jones, a minister and university dean, describes this practice as a dance with several steps:[3]

1. Become willing to speak truthfully and patiently about conflicts that have arisen.
2. Acknowledge both the existence of anger and bitterness and a desire to overcome them.
3. Summon up a concern for the well-being of the other as a child of God.
4. Recognize your own complicity in conflict, remember that you have been forgiven in the past, and take the step of repentance.
5. Make a commitment to struggle to change whatever caused and continues to perpetuate the conflicts.
6. Confess a yearning for the possibility of reconciliation.

We all need to be forgiven and to forgive. This practice of regular forgiveness releases negative emotions that we carry when we harbor animosity or anger—and which can lead to physical illness. Forgiving others brings us closer to them and to God. It also reminds us of our own sinfulness and helps us to remain humble and receptive to God's grace.

Worship. Worshiping regularly can be a particularly difficult challenge for those in public ministry. While there are times when a pastor can truly worship while leading the service, he or she is often distracted by the task of providing a meaningful worship experience for others. Finding a spiritual community that can provide regular opportunity for worship is important for nurturing your spiritual health. Perhaps you can get together with a small group from your congregation or with your staff. Or maybe you could worship with your peers at regular meetings. Maybe you could attend services at a Christian college or at another church in your community. Find your worship home and be a regular participant.

Sing praises. At a recent conference for pastors, I talked about the health benefits of singing. The combination of physical effort and controlled breathing along with the expression of emotion is a very healthy release. We agreed that a good prescription for community health would be to gather every morning in the center of the community to sing. Think about the sense of community and inspiration a school song provides. Imagine starting your day surrounded by your neighbors greeting the day in song! Maybe singing in the shower will have to do. Join a choir or at least sing the hymns with gusto!

Kent Groff writes of the discipline of the heart and mind that is needed in spiritual wellness. He also writes about imitating the model of living and teaching of Christ. He speaks of habits of the heart being formed and reformed:[4]

- Christ is re-presented through repeated acts in the liturgy of the community. Table grace, sermons, listening to scripture, experiencing baptisms, and breaking bread in communion stir our curiosity and help us find meaning.

- Creative ritual, repeating the stories we know so well with passion and love, helps keep faith alive.
- Faith is like a spiral staircase. We come around again and again to the same issues of doubt and faith but always at a deeper level.
- Repeating the Psalms is one of the ways the soul is kept clean before God, expressing its anguish and anger, joy and confidence.
- The four Gospels are meant to be read again and again. The repeated cycle of the Christian year reminds us that the risen Messiah continues to join us in our human journey from beginning to end.

Pray. Mother Teresa shared these wise words: "The beginning of prayer is silence. . . . God speaking in the silence of the heart. And then we start talking to God from the fullness of the heart. And he listens. The beginning of prayer is scripture. . . . We listen to God speaking. And then we begin to speak to him again from the fullness of our heart. And he listens. That is really prayer. Both sides listening and both sides speaking."[5]

Sabbath

> *Remember the sabbath day, and keep it holy. Six days you shall labor and do all your work. But the seventh day is a sabbath to the LORD your God; you shall not do any work.*
>
> Exodus 20:8–10

Wayne Muller, minister and therapist, writes in *Sabbath,* "Sabbath is more than the absence of work; it is not just a day off, when we catch up on television or errands. It is the presence of something that arises when we consecrate a period of time to listen to what is most deeply beautiful, nourishing, or true. It is time consecrated with our attention, our mindfulness, honoring those quiet forces of grace or spirit that sustain and heal us."[6] We tend to work every day, whether it is for our job or for our home and family. But maintaining spiritual health requires taking time to nourish the soul. Public ministry means being able to call upon spiritual resources when we are least able— when we are exhausted, angry, or sad—and when the need for spiritual rescue is a devastating event that is unfathomable.

Parker Palmer writes of the need to protect and provide encouragement for the soul:

> The soul is like a wild animal—tough, resilient, savvy, self-sufficient, and yet exceedingly shy. If we want to see a wild animal, the last thing we should do is to go crashing through the woods, shouting for the creature to come out. But if we are willing to walk quietly into the woods and sit silently for an hour or two at the base of a tree, the creature we are waiting for may well emerge, and out of the corner of an eye we will catch a glimpse of the precious wildness we seek.[7]

Remembering the Sabbath means not working, but it also means intentionally living in God's world and appreciating the beauty of life and the grace of God as miraculous and essential gifts. When we are busy with work, we cannot appreciate the beauty of a blue sky tossed with fluffy clouds, the sweet wake-up call of the birds in the early morning, or the warmth that fills us fully from the smiles of those who are precious to us. We do not take the time to have a meandering conversation with God about the world around us and our calling within it. It is not a selfish act, but a selfless one. We cannot fully serve our families, friends, congregation, or community if we are not renewed, refreshed, and reminded of our relationship with God.

Questions

1. How do you practice your faith?

2. How do you practice forgiveness?

3. When, where, and with whom do you worship?

Living Well

There is no state of perfect health. Although we strive for positive health through a healthy lifestyle and good self-care, death is inevitable and unpredictable, and many of us will be living with chronic illness. The goal then is to practice healthy behavior to prevent and delay illness or disability, but also to live well in the context of chronic illness, stressful environments, and in anticipation of death.

Prepare for Illness

*God creates new health in the midst of suffering, and even
when we are ill, God has a greater wholeness to offer us.*

—James Wind, *A Letter on Peace and Good Health*[1]

No one welcomes a diagnosis of a chronic or life-threatening illness. Sometimes there is no known cause for significant health problems, such as multiple sclerosis and some forms of cancer. Other illnesses run in families, for example, muscular dystrophy, colon polyps, and depression. Being familiar with the health issues that have affected your close family members is important so that you can understand your risk for specific diseases and what you can do to prevent or delay the onset. Knowledge about diseases in your family can help you take appropriate steps in planning your healthcare and in addressing the lifestyle behaviors that put you at higher risk for health problems. There are things you can learn and do to maximize your chance of living a healthy and active life.

If you know that you are at risk for certain diseases because of your family history or because of your own medical history, you have even more incentive to be aware of early symptoms and to intentionally act to lessen your risk. For example, if you know you may be prone to developing diabetes because you are an American Indian, have a strong family history of diabetes, or had diabetes in pregnancy, you will want to maintain a healthy weight and exercise regularly. If you have a personal history of depression or a strong family history of it, you will want to be aware of early symptoms of depression and seek professional help. In addition, you should seek balance in your life with a good diet, adequate rest, regular exercise, a social support system, and a healthy work environment.

Manage Your Illness

Many of us find that it takes a serious illness to get us to be serious about our health. While we may be too late to prevent injury or weakness that results from being seriously ill, we may still glean some positive results from our illness. For instance, a serious illness may strengthen our relationship with family members or with God. Sometimes it gives us the permission to change things that we have been unable to change. Sometimes it gives us the time to listen to our own hearts, to those who are closest to us, and to God.

Living well with chronic disease requires attention and effort from you and from your family. Day-to-day disease self-management means several things:

- engaging in activities that promote physical and psychological health

- interacting with healthcare providers and adhering to treatment recommendations
- monitoring health status and making associated care decisions
- managing the impact of the illness on physical, psychological, and social functions[2]

Being ill does not mean that you cannot live well. Being ill involves change and requires you to be ready for that change. Be aware of the impact of your disease over time. Be knowledgeable about your disease and its treatments. Have a plan and a support system—in your family and within your healthcare system. Make changes in your life to adapt to your illness but also to maximize your health. Use this life change as an opportunity to reevaluate what is important to you and how you might change your life to assure that you are living well.

Talk to your physician about managing your health. Ask for help or advice on diet and physical activity. Ask about resources to help you understand the impact of your disease and how you can prepare for or lessen the impact. Make it clear that you want to be involved in the decisions about treatment. Make sure that you have someone in your family who is also knowledgeable and can be helpful in guiding decisions or making decisions on your behalf. Ask if there are organizations that provide support or individuals who could share their success stories in living well with disease.

Dying Well

> *Even though our outer nature is wasting away, our inner nature is being renewed day by day. For this slight momentary affliction is preparing us for an eternal weight of glory beyond all measure, because we look not at what can be seen but at what cannot be seen; for what can be seen is temporary, but what cannot be seen is eternal.*
>
> 2 Corinthians 4:16–18

Henri Nouwen writes:

> Is death something so terrible and absurd that we are better
> off not thinking or talking about it? Is death such an undesir-
> able part of our existence that we are better off acting as if
> it were not real? Is death such an absolute end of all our
> thoughts and actions that we simply cannot face it? Or is it
> possible to befriend our dying gradually and live open to
> it, trusting that we have nothing to fear? Is it possible to
> prepare for our death with the same attentiveness that our
> parents had in preparing for our birth? Can we wait for our
> death as for a friend who wants to welcome us home.[3]

As Christians, our perspective on death and God's promise
of resurrection enable us to approach death with hope. As Americans, we do not plan for death; we go into denial. Nevertheless, we all must experience death, so we would be wise to take
time to prepare for it, even if it should come upon us un-
expectedly. And we also must prepare for the death of family
and friends. This means being aware that death is ever present.

Be mindful of your relationships—with God and with others. Communicate regularly through prayer, presence, writing,
and talking. Make your wishes known about how you might
want your body to be treated in the event that you are unable
to communicate; that is, make a "living will." You have a legal
right to accept or refuse treatment. Make it clear who can make
decisions on your behalf (a "healthcare proxy" or "durable
power of attorney" for healthcare). Creating an advance directive, a written document making your wishes known, is important, but it is just as important to let those who surround
you in your life know your desires and where those details are
documented.

Living with the knowledge that death is coming soon can be
a time of great clarity about what is most important in life. It is
a time to create precious memories for loved ones. It is a time to

leave a legacy of words, pictures, and presence. It is a time for expressing love to family and friends in ways that will surround them and provide comfort for many years. One way of doing this is with an ethical will. An ethical will is a document that shares important personal values and beliefs, important spiritual values, hopes and blessings for future generations, life's lessons, love and forgiving others and asking for forgiveness.[4]

Palliative care means caring for the whole person—body, mind, and soul—throughout the dying process. Dying is natural and personal, and the goal is to see that you have the best quality of life you can have at this time. The World Health Organization defines palliative care as an approach that improves the quality of life of patients and their families facing the problems associated with life-threatening illness, through the prevention and relief of suffering by means of early identification and impeccable assessment and treatment of pain and other problems, physical, psychosocial, and spiritual.[5]

Palliative care:

- provides relief from pain and other distressing symptoms
- affirms life and regards dying as a normal process
- intends neither to hasten nor postpone death
- integrates the psychological and spiritual aspects of patient care
- offers a support system to help patients live as actively as possible until death
- offers a support system to help the family cope during the patient's illness and in their own bereavement
- uses a team approach to address the needs of patients and their families, including bereavement counseling, if indicated
- will enhance quality of life, and may also positively influence the course of illness
- is applicable early in the course of illness, in conjunction with other therapies that are intended to prolong life, such as chemotherapy or radiation therapy, and includes those

investigations needed to better understand and manage distressing clinical complications

The Robert Wood Johnson Foundation report "Means to a Better End" suggests these five principles for palliative care:

1. respect the goals, likes, and choices of the dying person
2. look after the medical, emotional, social, and spiritual needs of the dying person
3. support the needs of the family members
4. help gain access to needed healthcare providers and appropriate care settings
5. build ways to provide excellent care at the end of life[6]

National Hospice Foundation research shows that 80 percent of Americans want to die at home surrounded by loved ones and free from pain. The reality is that Americans die in hospitals and nursing homes, in pain and hooked up to life-sustaining technology they do not want. Only 25 percent actually die at home. Hospice and palliative care are available today, but families need to know about it, ask for it, and make these plans with their loved ones in advance. Having the right care by trained professionals who are knowledgeable about the dying process, in a comforting environment at home or in a hospice setting, is a gift to the individual and to family and friends. Of the patients who receive hospice care, over 75 percent die at home.

A Prescription for Your Health

The ancient Hebrew regulations about cleanliness and godliness remind us that health must be incarnated in our daily life patterns and practices—and that our patterns and practices must be centered in a healthy relationship with God.

—James P. Wind, *A Letter on Peace and Good Health*[7]

Health is not the "absence of disease"—as Western medicine has defined it. Health and wellness are the balance of all aspects of health—physical, emotional, social, vocational, intellectual, and spiritual. One way to get started on the journey to health and wellness is to write out a personal prescription. Americans are accustomed to having health treatments prescribed and are more likely to be compliant with a written prescription. List each aspect of health from the Wholeness Wheel and write out a plan for each one. Be specific and include how much, how often, and for how long.

Think about where your life is out of balance and start there. Most of us can increase our physical activity level by planning a regular specific activity. For example, walk for 30 minutes 5 times a week. Eat 5 servings of fruits and vegetables daily. Maybe there is a book you would like to read that you have been putting off

---

My Prescription for Good Health
(How much, how often, for how long)

Name _____

Date _____

Physical

Emotional

Social/Interpersonal

Intellectual

Vocational

Spiritual

or a conference you want to attend. Read a new book once a month for the next year. Start regular meetings with your peers for spiritual enrichment or emotional support. Seek out a vocational mentor and plan regular meetings. Plan your vacation times for next year. Read a book of the Bible each week. Prescriptions are usually good for about one to three months. Plan to revisit your prescription and rewrite it to keep on the road to health and wellness.

Ten Best Practices for Health and Wellness

As Christians, we understand the value of rules to guide us in living a life of faith. Maintaining health and wholeness is essential in making the most of the life we were given. Here are some suggestions for being intentional about your health and wellness.

1. Love God with all your heart, soul, mind, and strength.
2. Love your neighbor as you *love yourself;* be an example of self-care as well as caring for others.
3. Remember the Sabbath and keep it holy; be intentional about time for rest and renewal within your week, church year, and life in ministry.
4. Honor your body as a gift from God and temple of the Holy Spirit. Feed it healthy foods, and build your physical and emotional endurance with regular physical activity.
5. Honor your mother, father, siblings, spouse, and/or children with your love, respect, and time.
6. Reflect your faith and use your gifts in your vocation.
7. Develop healthy habits to keep your Wholeness Wheel in balance and to be fit for a ministry of servanthood.
8. Equip yourself to use your gifts effectively to proclaim and live out the gospel in the world.
9. Practice and seek forgiveness.
10. Pray daily.

RL's Sabbatical

If ever there was an advertisement for sabbaticals, RL was it. It had been several months since I had last seen him. He had spent one month at a spiritual retreat center and two months at home reading, studying, and playing the piano. He had kept a spiritual journal and was excited to tell me about his experience.

"I feel so refreshed. I feel just like I did at my first installation, only better. I have the enthusiasm and the passion with the experience. I have so much hope for the future. I have established a wonderful routine of prayer every morning and journaling in the evening. It has really helped me keep that sense of peace that grew over my sabbatical. My sense of time has changed. The time pressure that I felt every day and the urgency that was ever present are gone. I have accepted that it's not my time, but God's time. I can do my best but only with God's help and with the support of others. I know that the challenge will be to keep this sense of peace and purpose. I am excited about the possibilities, though, and I'm really looking forward to the future.

"By the way, Deborah finished her first year of seminary and loved it. I am so proud."

Questions

1. Do you have a chronic disease? Are you at risk for one? How are you living well within that context?

2. Have you completed a living will or advanced directive? Have you talked with your family or friends about what is in it and where it is?

3. Knowing that death is inevitable, what would "dying well" mean for you?

4. Write a prescription for your health. Follow it. Share it with your family, friends, or physician.

Health and Wellness in Public Ministry

The 2002 *Pulpit & Pew* survey found that a large majority of pastors are satisfied with their vocation.[1] Six of ten have never doubted their calling, and seven of ten have never considered leaving pastoral ministry. For rostered leaders of the Evangelical Lutheran Church in America, the percent of satisfaction with job, calling, and vocation is above 90 percent. L. Gregory Jones suggests in an article in the *Christian Century* that one significant reason for that satisfaction may be the rich reward of sharing in the lives of other people.[2] He also suggests that there is a rhythm to ministry that echoes the rhythm of life: work, play, and rest; intimate relationships and a rich diversity of acquaintances; making joyful noise and being still; rigorous study and prayerful listening; and making a significant social difference yet in a quiet, hidden way.

Self-Care: Pastor or Physician

I don't really know what it is like to be in the shoes or the alb of a pastor. I have been an observer, as I am married to a pastor whose family includes several pastors. I do know, however, what it is like to be in a white coat and shoes that wear out from much use walking from room to room in the clinic and back and forth down hospital halls. Getting caught up in the passion and compassion of medicine is easy to do. It is a privilege to know the intimate details of many lives, to be with people at some of the most devastating and some of the most uplifting times of life. The rewards are great, for I get to be an integral part of someone's changing life and witness true miracles of faith. The burdens are heavy, for I sometimes feel inadequate to meet demands and needs that exceed my knowledge or energy.

Being a physician is a consuming role. Daily demands and details take up most hours. The unexpected—the mundane and the extraordinary, the secular and the sacred—can take days. Some days, I wear the white coat proudly—as a symbol of a profession that requires much education and training for a role that can have significant impact on a family or on a community. On other days, the white coat is just a garment to protect me from the mess of my day. Frequently I abandon the white coat for the anonymity of street clothes—a welcome relief to be simply another person walking down the street or eating fast food.

For some physicians, medicine is a prestigious job. They wear their white coats proudly and often and produce curricula vitae that weigh several pounds. For others, medicine is a calling—a vocation that uses their gifts and talents to provide a service to God and humanity. Physicians in the first category are vitalized and revitalized by accomplishments, reputation, and promotion. Balance may be an issue for them, but medicine is number one. Physicians in the second category are often vitally exhausted by giving more than they receive and by losing track of the balance in their lives that is the eternal spring of energy.

To be the best physician means to practice self-care. Physicians must recognize their own ills and must struggle with the remedies to understand the reality of their patients' lives. Physicians who don't practice the advice they frequently give their patients find it difficult to feel much integrity. Advice falls short if the patient recognizes it as being unrealistic or paternalistic. Struggling with our own issues of weight, stress, time management, family problems, chronic disease, or other challenges helps us to be effective in helping others. We must make time to eat regularly and healthfully, not just survive on coffee. We must make time for vacation and family and be present to fully enjoy that time—not worried about what is happening at the clinic or hospital.

We must also learn to work well in a team of health workers, whether in a clinic or hospital. The job of improving health and healing disease is a big one that cannot be accomplished by any one doctor. In fact, we have learned that we have a much greater effect on an individual or population if we work as a team in a system of care that is supported by evidence that what we are doing is effective. This has been a hard lesson to learn, as physicians are trained to believe that they are healers, following in the footsteps of their teachers or on the strength of their experience. As medical professionals, we constantly need to search for the truth and question what we do. Neither medical school nor seminary can prepare a person for living the life of a physician or a pastor. Because of the influence of our roles, it is vital that we be lifelong learners and grow personally and professionally.

Self-Care

The ordained minister needs to be an example of self-care, as well as caring for others. The significant demands of time and effort within the office of ordained ministry can lead one to neglect proper nutrition, exercise, and time for recreation. The congregation, or whatever agency or institution the ordained minister serves, should respect the need for the ordained minister to have adequate time for self-care. Caring for self also includes seeking counseling and/or medical care when there is evidence of physical or mental illness, substance abuse, eating disorders, or relational problems.[3]

Your health is not something that can be completely turned over to God or to your healthcare providers. Nor should it be something that gets attention only with the time you have left after addressing everyone else's needs. We read and hear about Jesus teaching, preaching, telling stories, healing, and leading by example. His work on earth is our example for public ministry. We also get glimpses of Jesus seeking and practicing health and wellness—physical, emotional, social, intellectual, vocational, and spiritual. We know that Jesus slept, ate, walked, wept, spent time with family, and went away to seek a quiet place. He cared tenderly for little children, he spoke to the disenfranchised and touched the unclean, he had pity on those who suffered, and he rebuked sinners. He spoke of love for his family, for his Father, for his disciples, and for the people of God. He taught others about the importance of love. He questioned the teachers in the temple and listened to and learned from them. He prayed, he sought counsel, and he gave counsel to others.

These aspects of Jesus' everyday life—physical, emotional, social, intellectual, vocational, and spiritual—may not be studied or preached about as often as other facets of his life, but they are an important part of the story. Jesus was practicing self-care to prepare for and to have strength for his journey of public ministry on earth. His needs were the needs of every human— food, rest, friendship, love, sense of purpose, and spiritual connection. His emotions were real, and his pain and hunger were real. He suffered exhaustion and isolation, and he endured unrealistic demands. Yet he knew how to practice self-care.

We all know the story of Jesus rebuking the stormy sea with the words, "Peace! Be still!" This stormy sea is a realistic picture of life in turmoil—seas constantly shifting and huge waves threatening, making you feel off balance, at risk, and somewhat sick. Kirk Jones writes of seeking out "the back of the boat."

> "The back of the boat" is a metaphor, a symbol of the necessary break from the activism of life, in general, and the rigor of ministry, in particular. The back of the boat is not a luxury. Time spent in the back of the boat is not optional if our intention is to lead a healthy, balanced, and productive life.

It is the back-of-the-boat time—the "off" time—that makes the bow-of-the-boat time—the "on" time—possible.[4]

We all need to make a habit of getting to the back of the boat for rest and recharging for our daily ministry.

Healthy Habits

Ministry is demanding physically, emotionally, socially, intellectually, vocationally, and spiritually. For those whose calling is clear and whose personal gifts are suited for ministry, positive health may be the outcome. For many in ministry, a lack of self-care and unreasonable personal or congregational expectations result in an imbalance that leads to poor health. Being responsive to expectations that include being faithful to Jesus Christ, knowledgeable of the Word of God and the confessions of the church, respectful of the people of God, and alert to the needs of a changing world requires balance and positive health. In turn, balance and positive health require self-care and the development of healthy habits. Healthy leaders enhance the lives of their families, congregations, communities, and the church. And being healthy as a congregation shows in worship, in meetings, and in outreach to the community. Healthy leaders bring energy, creativity, passion, and vitality to the church. In return, a vital church will attract new members and healthy and passionate leaders.

Here are some suggestions for healthy pastors/church leaders:

- Prepare your sermons while walking or riding a stationary bicycle.
- Pray while walking; consider a labyrinth.
- Schedule time for daily devotions, study, or prayer.
- Discuss and plan for a sabbatical.
- Consider taking small group meetings on a walk.
- Have health and wellness breaks during meetings.
  1. Have a healthy snack.
  2. Take a stretch break.
  3. Do relaxation exercises.
  4. Sing a rousing hymn.

- Take the stairs on hospital visits.
- Plan for regular meetings with peers for intellectual stimulation, emotional support, social enjoyment, and/or physical activities.
- Walk when you can to church, to home visits, to the hospital; or at least park farther away from your destination.
- Go home for a healthy lunch and a break during your day.
- Consider dividing your days into three sections (morning, afternoon, and evening) and working only two of the three.

Wellness Planning or Activities

Just as our church leaders need to attend to personal health and wellness, our congregations need to create a healthy environment and encourage health and wellness for everyone. Here are some suggestions:

- Create a wellness committee to address issues of health and wellness within the congregation, such as
    - educational opportunities
    - healthy food guidelines
    - appropriate and healthy times for meetings
    - healthy physical activities on a regular basis
    - use of the Wholeness Wheel to guide programming and opportunities
    - encouraging more movement in worship services
    - prayer resources
    - community-based activities
    - health ministries
- Invite healthcare workers in the congregation to be part of the ministry team.
- Consider health ministry as part of the mission of your congregation and a parish nurse as an integral part of that ministry.
- Create healthy church cookbooks.
- Put up a basketball hoop or soccer or volleyball nets and use them regularly.

- Start sacred dance classes, walking groups, sports teams, healthy cooking classes, activity nights, stress management classes.
- Add healthy topics or activities to adult and youth forum meetings.
- Plan for family events with the Wholeness Wheel in mind.
- Incorporate the Wholeness Wheel into Sunday school and confirmation.

Rev. Deborah L. Patterson, executive director of the International Parish Nurse Resource Center, shares the following information: Parish nurses can have a positive effect on the health and wellness of pastors, staff, and congregation by (1) sharing the load, (2) providing health education, (3) providing health assessment, (4) being supportive of healthy lifestyle changes, (5) making screening or preventive services convenient, and (6) helping to build up the volunteer base of the congregation to off-load tasks that could be done by people other than ordained clergy or staff.

Health and wellness are not just events or projects. They are a way of life, a cultural change. Making the decision to incorporate health and wellness into your church may take some planning and effort at the beginning, but it will become essential to the continued life of the congregation. It may become invisible within the planning, operations, and communications of the church, but it will be visible to everyone as a life-giving force that makes ministry and mission exciting.

Questions

1. What barriers have you experienced to practicing self-care? How have you overcome them?

2. What are your healthy habits? How have you managed to keep up healthy habits?

3. What successful healthy activities have you experienced in your congregation?

Boundaries

Trust is essential for pastors and church leaders. Ordained ministers bear the responsibility for faithful preaching, responsible teaching, and confidentiality in individual confession and counseling. It is that pastoral role that sets them apart from parishioners and church staff. To preserve that trustworthiness, it is necessary to keep appropriate professional boundaries and behavior. Thus it is important to maintain relationships outside the parish or congregation. Intimate relationships with family and friends are essential for emotional support and honest reflection. Collegial relationships with other clergy or other professionals in the community provide an appropriate outlet for frustration or doubt, for reflection on congregational issues, and for moral support and continued professional growth.

Isolation is one of the highest risk factors for illness or premature death. The 2001 survey showed that one in four of ELCA ordained clergy had a serious problem with friends or friendships in the past twelve months. Someone has suggested that the problem is that clergy have no friends. In a time when inappropriate sexual behavior by clergy appears rampant, the tendency is to avoid close relationships entirely. This is particularly true for single church leaders in smaller communities.

Sustaining supportive relationships is critical to good health. This means respecting and honoring your relationships with God and family. But that is not enough when so much of our time is spent at work. Being intentional about developing healthy relationships within the context of your congregation and your community is very important. Establish a ministry support committee with members who will be honest and emotionally supportive. Seek out other clergy or other professionals in the community outside the congregation for social and vocational support. Join social groups within the community for sports activities, art appreciation, musical performance, or other activities. While friendships inevitably develop in the context of a parish ministry over time, it is critically important to be clear at all times, with yourself and with the other person, when you are acting as a friend and when you are acting as his or her pastor. It is just as important to be aware of any inappropriate emotions or discomfort and deal with them immediately and honestly.

Lifelong Learning

> In an increasingly complex and educated society, the development of an informed intellect and professional skills is crucial to competent ordained ministry. This church expects of its ordained ministers regular and disciplined time for personal study, study in the company of others, participation in programs of continuing education, and periodic times for extended study.[5]

Vitality for attracting and retaining members and passion for providing for the spiritual needs of members and reaching out into the community come as a result of health and wholeness. Taking the time for directed learning in a way that challenges and expands your intellect and your knowledge is an essential step toward intellectual and vocational health.

The world has changed, the church has changed, and you have changed since your days at the seminary or other educational training. Continuing your education always brings renewal. You may find renewed passion for ministry, renewed understanding of the Word of God, or renewed relationships with other clergy, laypersons, or teachers who will continue to support your ministry.

Sabbatical

CHARIS Ecumenical Center at Concordia College in Moorhead, Minnesota, is one resource for sabbatical information. Regarding sabbaticals for pastors, CHARIS states:

A pastor is above all an authentic spiritual leader who has a number of specific tasks and roles, but underlying all of them is his or her role as spiritual leader. So what kind of sabbatical is appropriate for a spiritual leader? It probably needs to include components which permit time for reflection, for rekindling the spirit and the sense of calling by God, for reconnecting more deeply with the tradition (Scripture, theology, liturgy), and for deepening one's own spiritual life. It may also need to include time away from church things, time with family, or time alone.[6]

We know we benefit from taking a few days here and there for lifelong learning. We benefit from a change of scenery, using our minds differently, meeting new people, and renewing existing relationships. Public ministry is a very demanding vocation—personally and professionally. To remain engaged and active in the life of a congregation or in another form of ministry, we periodically need to make a more significant effort to disengage from day-to-day demands and immerse ourselves in seeking what we need personally to grow in ministry. Planning and preparing for a sabbatical is part of keeping your passion for ministry alive and keeping your gifts for ministry finely tuned. Sabbaticals don't just happen; you must plan for protected time away and gather resources to learn from. Furthermore, you will need to learn methods to keep the fresh perspective and vitality gained from sabbatical alive on your return. Families and congregations also need preparation for being supportive while you are on sabbatical and encouraging when you return.

Here are some helpful suggestions from CHARIS about how a sabbatical can help the congregation:

- A sabbatical can be a great time to develop lay leadership that might otherwise not step up because "the pastor does that." A well-planned sabbatical can be a great occasion for revisioning, reinvigorating, and recommitting lay leadership. For this very reason, it may be desirable not to seek a replacement, except for emergencies.

- A sabbatical can give the congregation and especially its leadership a much clearer picture of what actually happens in the congregation and what the pastor does.
- A sabbatical may be a time for the whole congregation to get into the "sabbath" mood—a distinctively countercultural stance of letting go and letting God, and rethinking the "busyness" of congregational, family, and individual life.
- The sabbatical can provide refreshed, reenergized pastoral leadership—and may well extend the "useful" life of the pastor.
- The sabbatical can be a means for the pastor to bring back new ideas gleaned from other churches to his or her own congregation.
- The congregation will benefit by letting the pastor experience life from the perspective of the pew, which can help the pastor sympathize with some of the concerns and assumptions of the people in the congregation.
- In some cases, the sabbatical may be a time for equipping the pastor for a new challenge or program chosen by the congregation.

Questions

1. How have you sustained healthy friendships? Talk or write about the value of those friendships to your ministry.

2. Talk or think about the growth in ministry or in life that you have experienced as a result of a lifelong learning experience.

3. How have you sustained the state of wellness following a sabbatical?

4. How have the experiences of sabbatical nourished your ministry?

Spiritual Growth

Helping others grow spiritually without tending to your own spiritual growth is difficult. The passion and vision for your ministry that led you to the seminary and were nurtured there cannot be sustained without attention. You must set aside time specifically for that purpose. This includes time for daily prayer or devotion, time for worship, and time for reading and/or writing that are not specifically for sermon preparation or church newsletters. Listening to or playing sacred music may be beneficial as well. And some ministers are enriched by group experiences or the help of a spiritual director.

Gary Harbaugh, a professor of pastoral care, reminds us that worship or personal devotion is our personal response to God's grace. He suggests answering some specific questions to better understand your personal spiritual path:

1. What is the heritage you bring to your spiritual response to God?
2. What connections can you make between your worship preferences and personal devotional practices and your gender, marital status, training or vocation, the presence or absence of children in your home, the stage in life you are going through, and any crisis you have experienced?
3. Is your response to God more action-oriented or more reflective?
4. Does structure help you worship?
5. What balance do you maintain between the ministry of the church and the mission of the church?[7]

The ELCA document "Visions and Expectations" reminds us that "the ordained minister is to nourish the people of God through the Word and sacraments. In order to do this, the ordained minister needs to develop and nurture a sound knowledge of the Scriptures, both intellectually and devotionally." Be thoughtful and intentional about your own spiritual growth that enables you to proclaim and live out the gospel within the church and in the world. Nourishing the people of God requires self-sustenance through regular personal nourishment from the Word of God, from regular communication with God, and from worshiping God in communion with others.

Sabbath

Then he said to them, "The sabbath was made for humankind, and not humankind for the sabbath."

Mark 2:27

God created the heavens and the earth and all that is in them, and rested on the seventh day. The commandment to remember the Sabbath has two purposes: rest/renewal and worship. Ministers are not excused from this commandment. The need to be rested and refreshed is essential to work in service to God and to God's people. Time is necessary to renew relationships with God, with family, with friends, with community, and with the earth. Spending a day doing holy things is what is expected. For some, being responsible for worship services is not always worshipful. For most, it is not restful. To keep the Sabbath holy means for ministers to set aside one day a week for rest, renewal, and holy activities.

Theologian Marva Dawn writes about Sabbath wholeness.

Our spirits become more unified when our relationship with God is the center and focus of our lives and all other aspects find their proper priorities in the worship of the Lord. Our bodies are more sound when we enjoy a rhythm of fasting and feasting, when we truly rest by giving up the burden of possessions, when we have time for naps. Our souls are more complete when we can get in touch with our deepest emotions, our true sexuality, our creativity, and our sense of delight and play. Our minds become more robust when the narratives of our heritage as God's people remind us of our redemption and when, as a result, our attitudes are made more wholesome and our freedom leads to the generating of new ideas. Furthermore, the interworking of all these aspects of our beings finds a new unity in Sabbath keeping because we no longer dichotomize between mind and matter, our bodies and our spirits or souls, our left and right brains. Rather, all becomes sacred and wholly integrated in our distinction from the world. We have even seen that there ceases to be any dichotomy between solitude and communal togetherness, because each is necessary for the other, and each contributes to the fullness of our being in relationship with God. As we become more intentional both about being a gathered Christian community and about enjoying our special times of solitude with God, the two work together to create a greater sense of both individual and corporate wholeness.[8]

Think about what brings you closer to God. It may be personal prayer and meditation in quiet solitude. Or it may be frolicking in nature and experiencing the gifts of God through sight, sound, smell, taste, and touch. Or it may mean worshiping with others in the colorful reflection of the sun's rays through stained glass, surrounded by beloved sacred music and the Word of God. Meaningful Sabbath is uniquely personal. It was created for us, but it does not happen without self-awareness and without intentional planning.

Pastor Mary

Pastor Mary is my own pastor. She and I meet periodically to share the stories of the stresses of a caring profession as well as the demands of balancing work with family. She and I both know the sacred privilege of being present for life and death and sharing the innermost thoughts and needs of others, and the absolute joy of witnessing miracles—small and large.

We both have felt the call to our vocations, although it

wasn't clearly named for us as young women. We knew that we had gifts given by God that we wanted to share with others in a caring profession. Life led Mary to the seminary and me to medical school. We shared stories of our families of origin—the good and the bad—and how they formed us into who we are today. We shared stories of experiences in our training and early years of ministry and medicine—stories of blatant discrimination or bemused tolerance. We shared our own struggles with how our gifts were best used, how to work with and play well with others in our work, how to survive ministry/medicine and child raising, and how grateful we are for the loving support of our husbands.

We know that as women we have helped to bring balance to male-dominated professions. We believe that it is healthy when the church and the profession of medicine reflect society in gender, race, and culture. We believe that medicine and ministry are often done best with a team that brings a wide variety of gifts and skills to meet a broad set of needs.

We have been blessed with many gifts and lessons that we have received from our parishioners and patients—lessons of love, patience, curiosity, leadership, piety, and humility. We have grown through mentorship, lifelong learning, modeling, teaching, self-care, grace, and prayer. We are grateful for every day we have to serve God and others. We are nourished by the love we receive from God and our families. We are grateful for each other.

Questions

1. Talk about a time of spiritual growth. How did it affect your ministry? How did it enhance your wellness?

2. What are your Sabbath practices? How are you renewed?

3. When and how do you converse with God?

The Gift of Ministry

10

We have gifts that differ according to the grace given to us: prophecy, in proportion to faith; ministry, in ministering; the teacher, in teaching; the exhorter, in exhortation; the giver, in generosity; the leader, in diligence; the compassionate, in cheerfulness.

Romans 12:6-8

Qualities of Good Ministers

Vocational health is the result of good training and lifelong learning practices, but it is also the result of making the right choice based on your personal qualities and gifts. Melissa Wiginton, director of the Ministry Program and Partnership for Excellence for the Fund for Theological Education, Inc. (FTE), gave a presentation in Indianapolis in January 2003.[1] At the FTE, she has studied the lives of young people who will become exceptionally good ministers and has found "markers of resistance" to the current culture of the ethic of accomplishment. They are:

1. an inner life: the capacity to be quiet and still long enough to access their inner lives
2. a sense of wonder: strengths based on artistry and exploration from experiences that hold the possibility of wonder, of self-transcendence
3. appreciation of ritual: needing to be reminded through ritual of the holy that is larger than our own lives
4. connection-making: risking the vulnerability of truth emerging out of mutuality
5. engagement for healing the world: being interested in changing the world

These qualities or "markers" reflect in different words the dimensions of the Wholeness Wheel and the ability to keep them in balance. Having spiritual health is reflected in the capacity for an inner life, the sense of the mystical, and the value of ritual to honor the sacred. Physical, emotional, social, vocational, and intellectual health in balance and surrounded by spiritual health enable and empower successful connecting and engagement that change the world.

While these may be important qualities for ministry, personal gifts, styles, and approaches to ministry are varied. That variety is of great value for spreading the Word of God and working toward the mission of the church in different settings with different people. It is important to understand your personal gifts and style and how you can use those gifts in the right setting to accomplish God's work in the world.

Congregational Expectations of Pastors

Just as personal gifts and fit to mission and ministry impact vocational health, so do the expectations of the congregation to which you are called or in which you are pastoring. Adair Lummis conducted interviews with lay leaders and judicatory executives to outline pastoral qualities sought by call committees.[2] They include the following:

- demonstrated competence and religious authenticity
- good preacher and leader of worship (lay leaders are concerned that this relates to their own lives and engages them personally)
- strong spiritual leader
- commitment to parish ministry and ability to maintain boundaries
- available, approachable, and warm pastor with good "people skills"

- male gender remains a criterion for most search committees—typically married men with children, under age forty, in good health, with more than a decade of experience in ministry
- consensus builder, lay ministry coach, and responsive leader
- entrepreneurial evangelists, innovators, and transformational reflexive leaders

The U.S. Congregational Life Study (April 2001) found some interesting results in comparing fast-growing congregations with randomly selected congregations. Fast-growing congregations were more likely to be described by attendees as currently moving in new directions, trying new things, anticipating the future, serving the wider community, serving children and youth, having a clear vision for mission that is supported by attendees, meeting the spiritual needs of attendees, and having attendees who are becoming more active and who invite family and friends to worship. Also, there was a good match between fast-growing congregations and pastors and other leaders who inspired people to take action, took into account worshipers' ideas, encouraged people to find and use their gifts, and taught people about their faith.

Unhealthy situations result when there is a gap between the congregation's expectations and the pastor's gifts and strengths or the pastor's perception of the congregation's needs. Open communication and healthy pastor/lay leader relationships are essential for a healthy pastor and congregation. At times consultation or facilitation is useful to define the gaps and help find ways to narrow them. Mentoring with successful experienced pastors who have been in similar situations or meeting regularly with a supportive group of colleagues to share ideas can be very healthy and helpful. Sometimes a pastor may find it necessary to acknowledge that the gaps are too wide and it is time to seek another call.

Practicing and leading others to practice healthy habits and balance of the Wholeness Wheel will shift the expectations of congregations positively. Conversations on difficult topics or on congregational mission change when viewed through the lens of health and wellness. Conflict will not go away, but working through conflict will become easier. Establishing expectations for healthy behavior and encouraging social gatherings for the purpose of improving health will build a healthy foundation for dealing with trauma or stress.

Change and Challenges

Our current existence is defined by constant change. Our lifestyles have changed as a result of technology that has changed the way we communicate and the way we work. Our culture has been impacted by political and economic changes, by violence and injustice, and by increasing cultural diversity. Changes in American culture, including the women's movement, gay pride, affirmative action, and an aging society have impacted the church. Conflict is common, whether about money, staff, worship style, music, ordination of homosexuals, or abortion. Change is stressful. Responding to change in a way that is productive without alienating most of your congregational members is essential. This requires time, energy, creativity, and strength.

Jackson Carroll, director of *Pulpit & Pew* Research on Pastoral Leadership, suggests three resources for ordained ministers to do good work:[3]

1. Resiliency: the combination of toughness and elasticity to endure challenges without breaking, grounded in God's grace
2. Agility: enables one to respond faithfully, innovatively, and appropriately in the face of a constantly changing world
3. Willingness to stay connected: being proactive in establishing appropriate friendships both within one's congregation and with fellow ordained ministers

Carroll reminds us that "It is God's ministry to which we are called, but it is also our ministry to keep vital and alive."

Responding positively to change is more likely to occur when there is stability in other dimensions of your life. Being grounded by a deep faith and in constant conversation with God gives us faith hardiness and enables us to "see with the eyes of faith."[4] Faith hardiness is that psychological trait of resilience to change or trauma that is strengthened by our knowledge that God is ever present. Having meaningful and supportive relationships is a stabilizing force. Seeking regular intellectual stimulation helps one to think creatively, or "outside the box." Seeking lifelong learning opportunities can create a network for connections while introducing skills or ideas to help manage change.

Leadership Style

Dealing effectively in the church with change or challenge requires effective leadership. How many of us have had the training or mentoring to develop a successful leadership style? How many of us have the insight to recognize leadership traits or weaknesses? Most of us probably expect that leadership comes naturally with time and experience or with inspiration from God. While certain gifts and personalities make for more effective leadership, being a truly effective leader comes from making the most of the gifts we have and matching personal leadership style to the culture or the needs of the congregation.

Pastor and leader Bill Hybels has written about different types of leadership style or, better, leadership gifts. One of the most successful qualities of a successful leader is knowing his or her personal gifts or style and how they impact the congregation. He describes these leadership gifts:[5]

1. *Visionary leaders* have a crystal-clear vision and a passion to see it accomplished.
2. *Directional leaders* have the ability to choose the correct path at critical intersections.

3. *Strategic leaders* form a game plan that organizes the players to succeed in realizing the vision.

4. *Managing leadership* can establish mile markers and organize people, processes, and systems to achieve a goal or mission.

5. *Motivational leaders* intuitively know who needs a fresh challenge, additional training, public recognition, an encouraging word, or a day off.

6. *Shepherding leaders* love and nurture team members, listening patiently and praying diligently so the team mission is achieved.

7. *Team-building leaders* have great insight into people, knowing who has the right abilities, character, and chemistry to create a team that will produce the right results.

8. *Entrepreneurial leaders* love the challenge of the impossible and function best in a start-up operation but do not do maintenance well.

9. *Re-engineering leaders* love to tune up health and revitalize hurting organizations.

10. *Bridge-building leaders* bring a wide variety of constituencies together under the umbrella of leadership to help a complex organization achieve its mission.

Knowing your gifts and leadership style is vital to understanding and accepting a call, but being a successful pastor may mean working at leadership skills that don't come naturally. Pastor Matthew Woodley writes about his experience as a shepherding leader trying to improve his administrative and leadership skills.[6] He makes the following suggestions:

1. Keep the congregation focused on their mission.

2. View your pastoral strengths as part of your unique style of leadership.

3. Make necessary decisions. Sometimes a leader must make a decision and weather the storm.

4. Ask crucial questions of the congregation. Raise issues and focus the discussion.

5. Communicate more. The congregation cannot read your mind.

Some differences in leaders and leadership styles may relate to age, experience, personality, gender, or ethnic background. These are legitimate differences that should be recognized simply as differences and not "wrong." The 2002 *Pulpit & Pew* study "Women's Path into Ministry: Six Major Studies" reviews the literature on women in ministry.[7] Lehman's study (1993) of ministry style in four mainline Protestant denominations reports that gender accounted for differences in the measure of four of nine areas:

1. More men than women manifested tendencies to use power over the lay members of the congregation.
2. More women than men were trying to empower their lay members to master their own spiritual lives and congregational affairs.
3. Men were more legalistic than women in dealing with ethical issues.
4. More men than women preferred making decisions using formal and rational criteria.[8]

Interestingly, pastoral role makes a difference. Copastors indicated fewer gender differences than clergy in more traditional appointments. For example, male copastors manifested the more feminine approach to ministry—rejecting the traditional masculine emphasis on preaching and opposing the traditional masculine clergy status system. Gender is more predictive of ministry style among senior pastors than among solo ministers. Among senior ministers, the men were more masculine and the women more feminine on six of the nine dimensions studied. The only areas where no significant gender differences appeared were approach to preaching, orientation to clergy status, and involvement in social issues. Clergy who graduated in the most recent cohort manifested more of the gender differences in ministry style discussed above, and among them additional differences emerged in interpersonal style and involvement in social issues. More women than men manifested open and vulnerable ways of interacting with lay members of their congregations, and women tended to be involved with social issues more than men.

There are many different gifts and styles of leadership. All are gifts from God, and when used for the glory of God, these different gifts enrich the lives of others through the Holy Spirit. Each one of us hears the Word of God differently and is receptive to different communication and teaching styles. Effective ministry is the result of healthy leadership and team ministry that combine the gifts and talents of a few to meet the many different needs of congregational members and a community.

Questions

1. How would you describe the qualities of a good minister?

2. Describe experiences you have had with a significant gap between the expectations of a congregation and a pastor. How was the gap addressed?

3. Describe how you have met the most significant change or challenge within your life of ministry. What skills or traits allowed you to cope successfully?

4. Describe your style of leadership and how it fits within your congregation or ministry.

The Gift of Ministry

If we could understand the factors behind the studies that showed that at one time Protestant clergy lived longer and healthier for almost every diagnosis when compared to others, public ministry would be the gift that keeps on giving.[9] Studies continue to show that people who do volunteer work in service to others live longer and have better physical and mental health. Harold G. Koenig suggests in his book *Purpose and Power in Retirement* that having a sense of meaning and purpose is what improves health. Many studies have also shown that "persons who are more involved in religious and spiritual practices experience greater well-being, life satisfaction, peace and hope, are more optimistic, more forgiving, more altruistic, less depressed and anxious, less likely to commit suicide, and generally live fuller and happier lives."[10] It appears that the calling to leave the world a better place is a reflection of health and wholeness.

Doing God's work in the world with the full experience of God's love and grace provides the ultimate sense of meaning and purpose. Accepting the call to do God's work has historically reaped the benefit of personal health and wellness. That very health and wellness liberate us to continue to love and serve others, and they are gifts that keep on giving. *Merriam-Webster Online* defines vocation as "a summons or strong inclination to a particular state or course of action; *especially* a divine call to the religious life." If we hear this summons and are able to bring our gifts and talents to public ministry or to ministry in daily life, we are receiving God's gift of life and Christ's gift of salvation. And we are giving to help others hear the summons and do the same. What has greater meaning than sharing the love of Jesus Christ with those who are able to receive and share that love with others?

Appendix: Wellness Guide

Name: _____

Date: _____

Age: _____ Height: _____

Physician's Name: _____

Physical Health Measures

Being Well	*Current Status*	*Goal Female (Male)*
Weight		BMI* 18.5–25
Waist measurement		F < 35 inches (M < 40 inches)
Blood pressure		< 120/80 Every two years if < 130/85
Cholesterol		Total < 200, HDL > 40 Optimal LDL < 100, NI < 130
Last Physical Exam		Age-based†
Immunizations		Age-based
Tetanus		Every 10 years
Pneumonia		Age 65

Physical Health Measures *(continued)*

Being Well	Current Status	Goal Female (Male)
Screening		
Pap smear		Every 3 years if normal
Mammogram		Every 1–2 years after age 40
PSA		Controversial, discuss with physician
Cholesterol		Every 5 years > 45 years (> 35 years)
Colon CA		After age 50 discuss method with physician
Prevention		
Sunscreen		Avoid sun, cover up, use sunscreen, wear sunglasses
No smoking		
No or limited alcohol		
Safe sex		Abstinence, monogamy, protection
Aspirin		At risk for heart disease, discuss with physician‡
Last dental visit		
Brushing		After each meal
Flossing		Daily

Physical Health Measures *(continued)*

Being Well	Current Status	Goal Female (Male)
Physical Activity		
Moderate physical activity		30 to 60 minutes daily§
Muscle strengthening		Twice a week
Flexibility/stretching		
Nutrition		
Meals		3—Breakfast, lunch dinner
Healthy snacks		2 to 3
Fruits and vegetables		At least 5 servings daily
Total calories		
Rest		
Sleep		7 to 8 hours a night
Relaxation exercises		Daily
Last vacation		Quarterly

*Body mass index—total weight in pounds divided by height in inches, and divided again by height in inches, multiply by 703.

†Specific attention to proper screening is more important than regular general physical exams.

‡ Daily aspirin may be recommended to reduce risk for heart disease, but there are risks.

§30 minutes are recommended for weight maintenance and prevention, 60 minutes for weight loss and health improvement.

Emotional Health

Being Well	*Current Status*	*Goal Female (Male)*
Recreational time		
Relaxation		
Stress coping skills		
Depression		In the past two weeks have you ever felt down, depressed, or hopeless? In the past two weeks have you felt little interest or pleasure in doing things? If yes, seek professional help.

Social Health

Being Well	*Current Status*	*Goal Female (Male)*
Significant-other time		
Communication		
Immediate-family time		
Communication		
Extended-family time		
Communication		
Friends time		
Communication		
Colleagues		

Intellectual Health

Being Well	*Current Status*	*Goal Female (Male)*
Education		
Continuing education		
Nonprofessional		
Mental exercise		

Vocational Health

Being Well	*Current Status*	*Goal Female (Male)*
Sabbatical		Every 7 years
Practical skills		
Leadership skills		
Communication skills		
Team-building skills		
Collegiality		

Spiritual Health

Being Well	*Current Status*	*Goal Female (Male)*
Prayer		
Devotions		
Study		
Worship		
Contemplation		

Living Well with Disease

Being Well	*Current Status*	*Goal**
Diabetes		
Weight		
Blood pressure		
Cholesterol		
Hgb A1C		
Monitoring labs/ studies		
Physical activity		
Last P.E. or clinic visit		
Foot exam		
Eye exam		
Diet		
No smoking		
Support system		
Heart Disease		
Weight		
Blood pressure		
Cholesterol/lipids		
Preventive medications		
Monitoring labs/ studies		
Physical activity		
Last P.E. or clinicvisit		
Diet		
No smoking		
Support system		

Living Well with Disease *(continued)*

Being Well	Current Status	Goal*
Cancer		
Weight		
Blood pressure		
Monitoring labs/ studies		
Last P.E. or clinical visit		
Physical activity		
Diet		
No smoking		
Arthritis		
Weight		
Exercise		
Injury avoidance		
Asthma		
Avoid triggers		
No smoking		
Osteoporosis		
Calcium/vitamin D		
Weight-bearing exercise		
No smoking		

Dying Well

	Current Status	*Goal*
Living Will (Advanced Care Directive)		
Completed		
Discussed		
Updated		
Accessible		
Ethical Will		
Completed		
Funeral Plans		
Completed		
Updated		
Palliative Care Plan		
Wants and desires		
Pain control		
Decision makers		
Family time		
Spiritual needs		
Caregivers		
Hospice Plan		
Decision makers		
Pain control		
Caregivers		
Environment of care		

Notes

1. Introduction

1. Gwen W. Halaas, *Ministerial Health and Wellness Report 2002,* for the Evangelical Lutheran Church in America (available at http://www.elca.org/dm/health/).

2. C. A. Rayburn et al., "Men, Women and Religion: Stress within Leadership Roles," *Journal of Clinical Psychology* 42, no. 3 (1986): 540–46.

3. The View from Pulpit & Pew: Provocative Findings on Pastoral Leading in the 21st Century. SACEM Presentation, February 21, 2003,5. See www.pulpitandpew.duke.edu.

4. H. King and F. B. Locke, "American White Protestant Clergy as a Low-Risk Population for Mortality Research," *Journal of the National Cancer Institute* 65, no. 5 (1980): 1115–24.

5. Ibid.

6. C. A. Rayburn et al., "Men, Women and Religion," 540–46.

7. P. J. Dewe, "New Zealand Minister of Religion: Identifying Sources of Stress and Coping Strategies," *Work and Stress* 1, no. 4 (1987): 351–63.

8. M. L. Morris and P. W. Blanton, "The Availability and Importance of Denominational Support Services as Perceived by Clergy Husbands and Wives," *Pastoral Psychology* 44, no. 1 (1995): 29–44.

9. Copyright the Inter-Lutheran Coordinating Committee on Ministerial Health and Wellness, Lutheran Church–Missouri Synod and Evangelical Lutheran Church in America, 1997.

10. Granger E. Westberg, *The Parish Nurse: Providing a Minister of Health for Your Congregation* (Minneapolis: Augsburg, 1990), 38.

11. Institute of Medicine, *Health and Behavior: The Interplay of Biological, Behavioral, and Societal Influences* (Washington, D.C.: National Academy Press, 2001), 1–4.

2. Physical Well-Being: A Health Body

1. From *Promoting Physical Activity: A Guide for Community Action* (U.S. Department of Health and Human Services, Public Health Service, Centers for Disease Control and Prevention, National Center for Chronic Disease Prevention and Health Promotion, Division of Nutrition and Physical Activity, Human Kinetics, Champaign, Ill., 1999).

2. United States Department of Agriculture and Department of Health and Human Services (food pyramid information at www.usda.gov).

3. Walter C. Willett, with P. J. Skerrett, *Eat, Drink, and Be Healthy* (New York: Simon & Schuster, 2001).

4. "Understanding Sleep: Brain Basics" (National Institutes of Health, National Institute of Neurological Disorders and Stroke) (available at http://www.ninds.nih.gov/health_and_medical/pubs/understanding_sleep_brain_basic_.htm).

5. Wayne Muller, *Sabbath: Finding Rest, Renewal, and Delight in Our Busy Lives* (New York: Bantam, 1999).

6. Shoni Labowitz, *God, Sex, and Women of the Bible: Discovering Our Sensual, Spiritual Selves* (New York: Simon & Schuster, 1998), 91.

7. R. E. Sieving et al., "Adolescent Sexual Behavior and Sexual Health," *Pediatrics in Review* 23, no. 12 (December 2002): 407–16.

3. Emotional Well-Being: A Healthy Mind

1. "Mental Health: A Report of the Surgeon General" (Rockville, Md.: U.S. Department of Health and Human Services, Substance and Mental Health Services Administration, Center for Mental Health Services, National Institutes of Health, National Institute of Mental Health, 1999), 4.

2. Chronic stress can also lead to vital exhaustion—another factor associated with susceptibility to heart disease. Vital exhaustion is a state of excessive fatigue, increased irritability, and demoralization. It is often associated with job stress. See Institute of Medicine, "Health and Behavior: The Interplay of Biological, Behavioral, and Societal Influences" (Washington, D.C.: National Academy Press, 2001), 2–16.

3. Ibid., 2–12.

4. J. O. Prochaska, J. C. Norcross, and C. C. Diclemente, *Changing for Good: A Revolutionary Six-Stage Program for Overcoming Bad Habits and Moving Your Life Positively Forward* (New York: Avon, 1994), 38–46.

5. B. Arroll, N. Knin, N. Kerse, "Screening for Depression in Primary Care with Two Verbally Asked Questions: Cross Sectional Study," *British Medical Journal* 327 (2003): 1144–46.

4. Intellectual Well-Being

1. R. Kolb and T. J. Wengert, eds., *The Book of Concord: The Confessions of the Evangelical Lutheran Church* (Minneapolis: Fortress Press, 2000).

5. Social/Interpersonal Well-Being: High-Quality Personal Relationships

1. J. P. Wind, "A Letter on Peace and Good Health" (Inter-Lutheran Coordinating Committee on Ministerial Health and Wellness, Evangelical Lutheran Church in America and Lutheran Church-Missouri Synod, June 23, 1998), 16.

2. Parker J. Palmer, *Let Your Life Speak: Listening for the Voice of Vocation* (San Francisco: Jossey-Bass, 2000), 30–31.

3. T. L. Campbell and S. H. McDaniel, "Family Systems in Family Medicine," *Clinical Family Practice* 3, no. 1 (2001): 13–33.

4. Shoni Labowitz, *God, Sex, and Women of the Bible: Discovering Our Sensual, Spiritual Selves* (New York: Simon & Schuster, 1998),120.

5. Ibid.

6. Mother Teresa, *Words to Love By . . .* (Notre Dame, Ind.: Ave Maria Press, 1983), 15.

7. Harold G. Koenig, *Purpose and Power in Retirement: New Opportunities for Meaning and Significance* (Philadelphia: Templeton Foundation Press, 2002), 86–89.

8. Kent Ira Groff, *Active Spirituality: A Guide for Seekers and Ministers* (Bethesda, Md.: Alban Institute, 1993), 140–49.

6. Vocational Well-Being

1. Parker J. Palmer, *Let Your Life Speak: Listening for the Voice of Vocation* (San Francisco: Jossey-Bass, 2000), 4.

2. Ibid., 5.

3. Ibid.

4. Joan D. Chittister, *Wisdom Distilled from the Daily: Living the Rule of St. Benedict Today* (San Francisco: Harper, 1990), 92–93.

7. Spiritual Well-Being

1. Harold G. Koenig, *The Healing Power of Faith: Science Explores Medicine's Last Great Frontier* (New York: Simon & Schuster, 1999), 24.

2. Debra K. Farrington, *Living Faith Day by Day: How the Sacred Rules of Monastic Traditions Can Help You Live Spiritually in the Modern World* (New York: Berkley, 2000), 175–79.

3. See his chapter, "Forgiveness," in Dorothy C. Bass, ed. *Practicing Our Faith: A Way of Life for Searching People,* 133–48 (San Francisco: Jossey-Bass, 1997), 138–39.

4. Kent Ira Groff, *Active Spirituality: A Guide for Seekers and Ministers* (Bethesda, Md.: Alban Institute, 1993), 122–24.

5. Mother Teresa, *Words to Love By* . . . (Notre Dame, Ind.: Ave Maria Press, 1983), 40.

6. Wayne Muller, *Sabbath: Finding Rest, Renewal, and Delight in Our Busy Lives* (New York: Bantam, 1999), 8.

7. Parker J. Palmer, *Let Your Life Speak: Listening for the Voice of Vocation* (San Francisco: Jossey-Bass, 2000), 7–8.

8. Living Well

1. James P. Wind, "A Letter on Peace and Good Health" (Inter-Lutheran Coordinating Committee on Ministerial Health and Wellness, Evangelical Lutheran Church in America and Lutheran Church–Missouri Synod, June 23, 1998), 35.

2. E. A. Bayliss et al., "Descriptions of Barriers to Self-Care by Persons with Comorbid Chronic Disease," *Annals of Family Medicine* 1, no. 1 (May/June 2003), 15–21.

3. Henri J. M. Nouwen, *Our Greatest Gift: A Meditation on Dying and Caring* (San Francisco: HarperSanFrancisco, 1994), xii–xiii.

4. This is a historical concept brought to our attention again by Barry Baines, a family physician. See ethicalwill.com.

5. The definition can be found at the World Health Organization's website: www.who.int/cancer/palliative/definition/en/.

6. Robert Wood Johnson Foundation, "Means to a Better End: A Report on Dying in America Today" (Washington, D.C., November 2002). See also lastacts.org.

7. Wind, "Letter on Peace and Good Health."

9. Health and Wellness in Public Ministry

1. The View from Pulpit & Pew: Provocative Findings on Pastoral Leading in the 21st Century. SACEM Presentation, February 21, 2003,5. See www.pulpitandpew.duke.edu.

2. L. Gregory Jones, "A Satisfying Vocation?" *Christian Century,* August 14–27, 2002.

3. "Vision and Expectations: Ordained Ministers in the Evangelical Lutheran Church in America" (Chicago: Division for Ministry, ELCA, 1990).

4. Kirk Byron Jones, *Rest in the Storm: Self-Care Strategies for Clergy and Other Caregivers* (Valley Forge, Pa.: Judson, 2001), 26.

5. ELCA, "Vision and Expectations."

6. CHARIS Ecumenical Center; Lifelong Learning Opportunities, Concordia College, Moorhead, Minnesota (www.cord.edu/dept/charis).

7. Gary L. Harbaugh, *The Confident Christian: Seeing with the Eyes of Faith* (Minneapolis: Augsburg Fortress, 2000), 130–32.

8. Marva J. Dawn, *Keeping the Sabbath Wholly: Ceasing, Resting, Embracing, Feasting* (Grand Rapids: Eerdmans, 1989), 137–38.

10. The Gift of Ministry

1. Melissa Wiginton, "Who Should Be Our Pastors?" *Pulpit & Pew* (Indianapolis, Ind.: Fund for Theological Education, January 8, 2003). See also http://www.pulpitandpew.duke.edu/wiginton.html.

2. A. T. Lummis, "What Do Lay People Want in Pastors? Answers from Lay Search Committee Chairs and Regional Judicatory Leaders," *Pulpit & Pew* (2002). See also pulpitandpew.duke.edu.

3. Jackson Carroll, "Leadership in a Time of Change," *Circuit Rider* (July/August 2002).

4. Gary L. Harbaugh, *The Confident Christian: Seeing with the Eyes of Faith* (Minneapolis: Augsburg Fortress, 2000), 14.

5. Bill Hybels, "Finding Your Leadership Style," *Christianity Today Leadership Journal* (winter 1998).

6. Matthew Woodley, "Good Pastor, Lousy Leader," *Christianity Today Leadership Journal* (Summer 1999).

7. E. C. Lehman Jr., "Women's Path into Ministry: Six Major Studies" (Duke Divinity School, Durham, N.C.: *Pulpit & Pew* Research Reports, no. 1 [Fall 2002]).

8. Edward C. Lehman Jr., *Gender and Work: The Case of the Clergy* (Albany, N.Y.: State University of New York Press, 1993).

9. H. King and F. B. Locke, "American White Protestant Clergy as a Low-Risk Population for Mortality Research," *Journal of the National Cancer Institute* 65, no. 5 (1980): 1115–24.

10. Harold G. Koenig, *Purpose and Power in Retirement: New Opportunities for Meaning and Significance* (Philadelphia: Templeton Foundation Press, 2002).

For Further Reading

Health and Healing

Bittner, Vernon J. *You Can Help with Your Healing: A Guide for Recovering Wholeness in Body, Mind, and Spirit.* Minneapolis: Augsburg, 1993. Uses the twelve-step process, with a study guide.

Callahan, Kennon. *Twelve Keys for Living: Possibilities for a Whole, Healthy Life.* San Francisco: Jossey-Bass, 1998.

McDaniel, Thomas R. *Dr. Luke's Prescriptions for Spiritual Health.* Carlsbad, Calif.: Magnus, 2000. A theological perspective on health and healing.

Nouwen, Henri J. M. *The Inner Voice of Love: A Journey through Anguish to Freedom.* New York: Doubleday, 1998.

Wind, James. "A Letter on Peace and Good Health." Inter-Lutheran Coordinating Committee on Ministerial Heath and Wellness. Evangelical Lutheran Church in America and Lutheran Church–Missouri Synod, June 23, 1998.

Physical Health

Chilstrom, Herbert W., and Lowell O. Erdahl. *Sexual Fulfillment for Single and Married, Straight and Gay, Young and Old.* Minneapolis: Augsburg, 2001.

Kesten, Deborah. *Feeding the Body, Nourishing the Soul: Essentials of Eating for Physical, Emotional and Spiritual Well-Being.* Berkeley, Calif.: Conari Press, 1997.

———. *The Healing Secrets of Food: A Practical Guide for Nourishing Body, Mind, and Soul.* Novato, Calif.: New World Library, 2001.

Kortge, Carolyn Scott. *The Spirited Walker: Fitness Walking for Clarity, Balance, and Spiritual Connection.* San Francisco: HarperSanFrancisco, 1998.

Northrup, Christiane, M.D. *Women's Bodies, Women's Wisdom: Creating Physical and Emotional Health and Healing.* New York: Bantam, 1994.

Rediger, G. Lloyd. *Beyond the Scandals: A Guide to Healthy Sexuality for Clergy.* Minneapolis: Fortress Press, 2003.

Sabbath/Sabbatical

Bullock, A. Richard, and Richard Bruesehoff. *Clergy Renewal: The Alban Guide to Sabbatical Planning*. Bethesda, Md.: Alban Institute, 2000.

Dawn, Marva J. *Keeping the Sabbath Wholly: Ceasing, Resting, Embracing, Feasting*. Grand Rapids: Eerdmans, 1989.

Muller, Wayne. *Sabbath: Finding Rest, Renewal, and Delight in Our Busy Lives*. New York: Bantam, 1999.

Self-Care

Harbaugh, Gary L. *The Confident Christian: Seeing with the Eyes of Faith*. Minneapolis: Augsburg, 2000. Includes a faith-hardiness inventory.

———. *Pastor as Person: Maintaining Personal Integrity in the Choices and Challenges of Ministry*. Minneapolis: Augsburg, 1984. Presents a holistic model of the physical, thinking, feeling, relating, and choosing person.

Melander, Rochelle, and Howard Eppley. *The Spiritual Leader's Guide to Self-Care*. Bethesda, Md.: Alban Institute, 2002. A fifty-two-week program in seven sections: 1. Creating a Life Vision, 2. Caring for Yourself at Work, 3. Nurturing Your Relationships, 4. Caring for Your Spirit and Body, 5. Caring for Your Finances, 6. Caring for Your Intellect, 7. Sustaining a Life Vision. Includes connecting with yourself, with a partner, and with God.

Oswald, Roy. *Clergy Self-Care: Finding a Balance for Effective Ministry*. Bethesda, Md.: Alban Institute, 1991. Includes self-care strategies.

Rediger, G. Lloyd. *Fit to Be a Pastor: A Call to Physical, Mental and Spiritual Fitness*. Louisville: Westminster John Knox, 2000.

Spiritual Health

Arnold, Johann Christoph. *Seeking Peace: Notes and Conversations along the Way*. Farmington, Pa.: Plough, 1998.

Bass, Dorothy C., ed. *Practicing Our Faith: A Way of Life for a Searching People*. San Francisco: Jossey-Bass, 1997.

Chittister, Joan D. *Wisdom Distilled from the Daily: Living the Rule of St. Benedict Today*. San Francisco: Harper, 1990.

Farrington, Debra K. *Living Faith Day by Day: How the Sacred Rules of Monastic Traditions Can Help You Live Spiritually in the Modern World*. New York: Berkley, 2000.

Groff, Kent Ira. *Active Spirituality: A Guide for Seekers and Ministers*. Bethesda, Md.: Alban Institute, 1993.

Norris, Kathleen. *The Cloister Walk*. New York: Riverhead, 1996.

Spirituality and Health

Koenig, Harold G. *The Healing Power of Faith: Science Explores Medicine's Last Great Frontier.* New York: Simon & Schuster, 1999.

Levin, Jeff. *God, Faith, and Health: Exploring the Spirituality-Healing Connection.* New York: Wiley, 2001.

Vocation

Erdahl, Lowell O. *10 Habits for Effective Ministry: A Guide for Life-Giving Pastors.* Minneapolis: Augsburg, 1996.

Everist, Norma Cook, ed. *Ordinary Ministry, Extraordinary Challenge: Women and the Roles of Ministry.* Nashville: Abingdon, 2000.

Hershey, Terry. *Soul Gardening: Cultivating the Good Life.* Minneapolis: Augsburg, 2000.

Kushner, Harold S. *Living a Life That Matters: Resolving the Conflict between Conscience and Success.* New York: Knopf, 2001.

Palmer, Parker J. *Let Your Life Speak: Listening for the Voice of Vocation.* San Francisco: Jossey-Bass, 2000.

Sitze, Bob. *Not Trying Too Hard: New Basics for Sustainable Congregations.* Bethesda, Md. Alban Institute, 2001.

Websites

www.4women.gov. Health information that is geared specifically for women's concerns.

www.ethicalwill.com. Ethical wills are a way to share your values, blessings, life's lessons, hopes, and dreams for the future, love and foregiveness with your family, friends, and community.

www.healthfinder.gov. Information about health and diseases.

www.lastacts.org. Last Acts is a national coalition of organizations engaged in an unprecedented education campaign to improve care for people who are dying and for their families.

www.mayoclinic.com. The website of the Mayo Clinic is a great resource for a wide variety of health-related issues.

www.partnershipforcaring.org. Partnership for Caring: America's Voices for the Dying.

www.sdiworld.org. Spiritual Directors International. Support and networking website for spiritual directors.

About the Author

Gwen Wagstrom Halaas is a family physician who has practiced family medicine for more than 15 years in St. Paul, Minnesota. Her practice included the full range of family medicine, including delivering babies, making house calls, and treating and counseling patients with depression and other stress-related disorders. She has been in medical education since 1986; most recently she directed the family practice residency training program at Regions Hospital in St. Paul, Minnesota. This included the teaching of health and wellness, management of disease, medical ethics, and assessing the health of communities. Prior to that she was a medical director for HealthPartners, a healthcare system in Minneapolis. There she was responsible for health plan policy decisions and was part of a quality management team. As medical director for UCare, a Medicaid managed care organization, she developed a health promotion/ disease prevention strategy for the members. She received her medical degree from Harvard Medical School and a Masters in Business Administration in Medical Group Management from the University of St. Thomas. She was an undergraduate at Concordia College in Moorhead, Minnesota.

Gwen was named project director for the Evangelical Lutheran Church in America's (ELCA) Ministerial Health and Wellness program by the Division for Ministry and the ELCA Board of Pensions. She began her work July 1, 2001. She is also Assistant Professor at the University of Minnesota Medical

School and associate director of the Rural Physician Associate Program.

Gwen is profiled in Fitzhugh Mullan's book, *Big Doctoring in America: Profiles in Primary Care* published by University of California Press, Berkeley. This is a book of the oral histories of 15 primary care practitioners who have practiced big doctoring described by Dr. Mullan as humanist, comprehensive, efficient and flexible, doctoring that builds on the legacy of the past and the rich tradition of care in medicine and nursing.

In addition to *The Right Road*, Gwen has authored two more books: *Living Well in Retirement* is forthcoming from the Alban Institute in 2004. The third, *On Call: Called to Serve*, is not yet published.

Gwen is married to the Rev. Mark W. Halaas, senior pastor at Christ Lutheran Church in Lake Elmo, Minnesota. They have three young adult children, Per, Liv, and Erik.

CPSIA information can be obtained at www.ICGtesting.com
Printed in the USA
245289LV00004B/31/P